Elena Bulatova

Throughput Computer Aided Design of Clothing and Accessories

Elena Bulatova

Throughput Computer Aided Design of Clothing and Accessories

Solving the problem of connection between the stages of modeling and design

ScienciaScripts

Imprint

Any brand names and product names mentioned in this book are subject to trademark, brand or patent protection and are trademarks or registered trademarks of their respective holders. The use of brand names, product names, common names, trade names, product descriptions etc. even without a particular marking in this work is in no way to be construed to mean that such names may be regarded as unrestricted in respect of trademark and brand protection legislation and could thus be used by anyone.

Cover image: www.ingimage.com

This book is a translation from the original published under ISBN 978-3-8443-5028-9.

Publisher:
Sciencia Scripts
is a trademark of
Dodo Books Indian Ocean Ltd., member of the OmniScriptum S.R.L Publishing group
str. A.Russo 15, of. 61, Chisinau-2068, Republic of Moldova Europe
Printed at: see last page
ISBN: 978-620-3-05323-4

CONTENTS

INTRODUCTION

Competitive apparel production is impossible without extensive automation at all stages of the cycle: planning   -
planning - planning - planning - planning - planning.
design - production - product sales. A modern fashion designer should be fluent in both computer graphics programs and computer-aided design (CAD) systems for clothes. Thus it is necessary to be guided in set of CAD clothes existing in the market. The existing systems differ significantly in their basic principles   and
technological capabilities   ,
productivity, accuracy of construction, necessary number of workplaces and peripheral equipment to perform the same work, ease of use and reliability, ease of learning and prospects for development.

At the enterprises which use computer technologies at designing of new models of clothes, now various graphic programs in which designers create sketches or technical drawings of new models are applied. On the created drawings of models designers of clothes also in CAD of different manufacturers develop drawings and patterns of details of projected products.

When designing models for industrial development, there is a problem of transition between the stages of modeling and design. The problem can be solved by introduction of essentially new process - the through automated designing of products from drawing of model to a design and modeling of its details. The development of through design technology was possible on the basis of CAD "Grazia". CAD "Grazia" allows not only to carry out any calculations and graphical constructions necessary both for designing of clothes, and for creation of a drawing - drawing of its appearance, but also in parallel unambiguously to write down all process (algorithm), with possibility of its reading, editing, copying.

I have been doing this work for more than 10 years, as I am interested and I am sure it will be in demand in due time. I would like to see this time come soon.

I would like to express my sincere gratitude to Lyudmila Mikhailovna Gladkova and Olga Viktorovna Zhuravleva, who together with me started developing through algorithms. I also thank the developers of CAD "Grazia" headed by Candidate of Physical and Mathematical Sciences Vitaly Grigorievich Eschenko, who gave us the opportunity to work with this wonderful system and take into account our comments and wishes in the constant improvement of the system.

1. DESIGN FEATURES OF INDUSTRIAL SEWING PRODUCTS AND GARMENT SAMPLINGS

Clothing should provide aesthetic and utilitarian functions. The process of its creation can be considered as artistic design, taking into account consumer requirements: conformity of clothes to the purpose, size, shape, fashion direction, etc.

Industrial production of products requires engineering design. The efficiency of production depends largely on the right choice of solutions at this stage. Products of mass production must meet not only consumer requirements, but also production - technological, economic.

The uniqueness of the clothing industry is that, unlike most other products of industrial production, clothing is most tied to the individual characteristics of consumers. It should:

- provide a good static and dynamic match to the figures of different physiques;

- are produced in different age and sex groups with a large number of models, differing in design and technological solution;

- are made of materials with a huge variety of properties;

- to be issued, as a rule, in small batches and promptly updated according to the fashion and consumer demands.

Due to the complexity of the tasks to be solved, modern industrial design of clothes is impossible without process automation.

At the Soviet enterprises of light industry, the first CAD patterns and layouts of clothing details appeared in the mid-eighties of the twentieth century. These were very expensive systems of the leading companies in this field: "Gerber" (USA), "Lectra" (France), "Investronika" (Spain). Then CAD of other foreign and domestic manufacturers appeared in the market. At the enterprises that have mastered computer technologies, quickly felt their advantages, and the return to traditional methods of work there has become unthinkable.

Soviet systems could not compete with foreign ones due to the lack of comparable capabilities and reliability of computing equipment. When modern personal computers and peripherals became widely available, various CAD systems started to develop rapidly in the post-Soviet space (Russia, Ukraine, Belarus).

As in other fields of activity, the purpose of automation is to perform the technical part of work quickly and qualitatively, leaving the creative part of the work to the person.

Designing of products should not end with working out of the design documentation as the maximum effect from automation can be received, only considering a problem from positions of the system approach. Thus system should be understood as designing, manufacture, sale. That is well developed CAD should:

-        Cover all stages of design and preparation of the model for production: creation of drawing of the model and its coloristic solutions (in knitting production and control programs for knitting machines), development of design documentation and layouts of patterns (when using automated cutting machines - control cutting programs), rationing of raw materials and materials, product technology, making and calculation of the technological process, the performance of economic calculations (up to the determination of the cost of the product);

-    generate information about the readiness of the model for launch, its passage in production and at the warehouse of finished products, on shipment to customers, as well as to perform implementation analysis for operational planning and production management.

This work is devoted to the development of technology for end-to-end automated processes of modeling and design of products, so the other stages of design, accounting, control and planning of production are not considered here. For ease of reference, the term "design" will refer to the stages of modeling and design. **Under through automated design is understood the process of creating in CAD parametric drawing-drawing of a new model of a certain cut by setting the values of parameters that characterize it, and automatic construction of structural details and their patterns.**

In order to analyze the existing ways of automating the processes of designing new models of clothing, first consider how it happens in the traditional (manual) process.

2. THE PROCESS OF NEW MODEL DEVELOPMENT WITH MANUAL IMPROVISATION

At the modeling stage, the artist (designer) creates a drawing of the future model. It can be a creative sketch reflecting the idea, the image of the designed product. But usually a sketch is not enough for the development of the design, because many design parameters on it may not be clear. More informative for the designer is a competently made technical drawing of the model, on which the product is shown (for the majority of products it is desirable on the figure) in the required proportions, with all design features.

The design phase of a product usually begins with the study and analysis of the model. Sometimes it is necessary to repeat an already finished model represented by a sample or a photo. In these cases, the designer should have a maximum of 7 faithfully replicate an already created product. But most often the designer deals with a creative sketch or a technical drawing of the model. Work with a drawing is one of the stages of the process of designing a new model. In this case, the design parameters and the product technology are determined, which may lead to the drawing correction. Its final specification can take place at performance of layouts or a sample of the product.

The design of the model of clothes can be obtained by different methods: by cartoon method, by calculation and graphic method or their combination.

The mummy (mock) method is most organized for the creative nature of the artist, as it allows you to directly create a model ("mold") of the material on a dummy or figure. In this case, the initial idea can be significantly transformed or fundamentally change due to the material features that are identified in the process of work. This method is indispensable when developing products with new shapes or when using materials with new properties. However, it is quite time consuming, requires some experience. In addition, the preparation for mass production of products on the basis of a sample obtained by the layout method, presents certain difficulties. This is largely due to the fact that the patterns of details should be developed on the finished product, taking into account the performed processing (planting, stretching, plotting, etc.). It is often very difficult to accurately reproduce all the nuances of obtaining a shape.

Therefore, the cartoon method is not used so often, usually by the calculation method first build the basic structure of the model (BO). Under BC is accepted to understand the drawings and patterns of the basic details of the base cut with specific values of composite (silhouette) additives. The basic cut of the shoulder products involves a sleeve sleeve, in this regard, the main details are considered: back, shelf (in front), sleeve. BO design can be obtained by any method, most importantly, it must be well "sit" (have a defect-free fit   )   on a typical   or individual figure. For reception of a design of projected model (a model design - MK) a base basis is modified by methods of constructive modelling.

3. WAYS TO AUTOMATE THE STAGES OF MODELING AND DESIGN OF CLOTHES

The most difficult in the design of new models of clothing is the transition from a sketch of the future model to its design. At this stage, in addition to the qualification of specialists who create the model - the artist (designer) and the designer, requires their absolute understanding, including tolerance to each other. As sometimes minor, from the point of view of the designer, deviations from the idea of the artist in the constructive parameters, which, moreover, can not always be caught on the sketch, violate the compositional integrity of the image, its harmony. This applies to the values of silhouette additions, configuration, location of decorative and structural lines, etc. Sometimes one's own mistakes become obvious to the artist when he sees a product designed exactly from the sketch on a real typical figure. In order to create a model that meets all the requirements of the artist, the designer and craftsmen sewing samples have to redo, and sometimes repeatedly, their work.

That is why the author has set a task: on the basis of CAD to create a technology that allows to automate the technical component of the processes of creating a drawing of the model and the development of its design and provides a direct link between these stages.

However, despite the current abundance of CAD clothing on the market, most of them can not serve as a basis for the development of technology end-to-end design. The solution of this problem was possible in CAD "Grazia".

For visualization of features of CAD "Grazia", distinguishing it from other CAD clothes, let's consider, how stages of studied process are automated in various CAD. The diagram (Fig. 1) shows the stages of clothing design (stages of modeling - design) and existing ways of their automation. Dotted line - no direct connection. The bold line highlights the principles of these stages, implemented in CAD "Grazia".

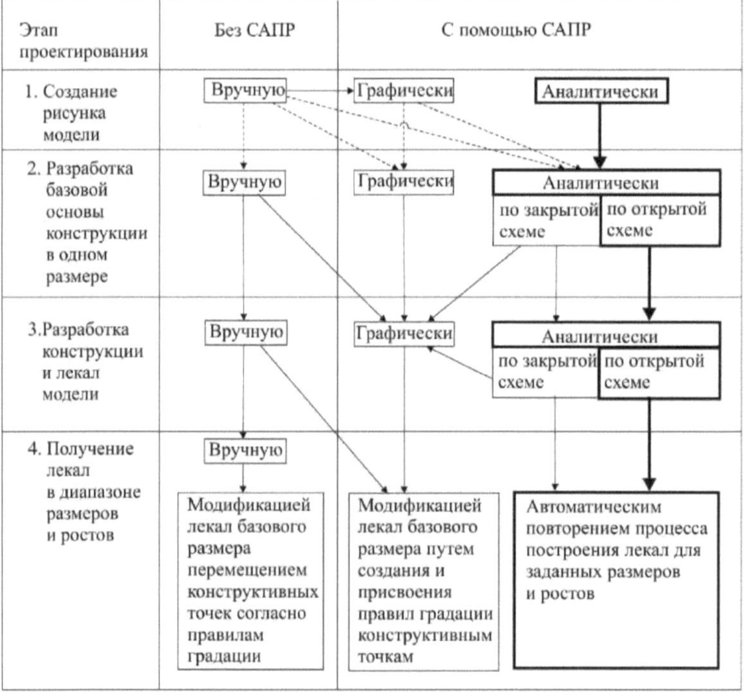

Fig. 1. Modeling-constructing stages of clothes and ways of their automation

When automating the modeling and design stages, the model drawing, construction drawings and patterns of product details are graphic information that can be entered into CAD from the manually made original using various peripherals (scanner, digital camera, digitizer) or created directly in the computer. As you can see from the diagram, there are two ways to get (task) graphic information about design objects in CAD:

- Direct creation of points and lines with the help of graphic tools;

- analytical description of graphic constructions. In the analytical method, the description of constructions can be accompanied by a parallel graphical display of the performed actions, can be created automatically when performing graphical actions. It is also possible to combine graphical and analytical methods at different design stages.

Working in ***graphical mode*** is essentially a drawing, drawing, not construction. For example, the famous universal drawing system AutoCAD is a classic graphic drawing system. It is simple enough to obtain drawings of details by creating points, connecting them with lines, drawing circles, and so on. In doing so, the user sets the desired distances, radii, and so on. The system considers the received points and lines as drawing, i.e. there is no possibility of parametrization, repetition of the drawing process with other values, and the more so of definition of these values by any formulas as it is done at clothes design. Besides, it is impossible to change the previously performed actions without destroying the results of the next ones.

The necessary accuracy, unambiguousness of the processes of calculation and drawing of the clothes construction can be achieved only with ***their analytical recording***. The design methods always give analytical description: source data, point and line designations, formulas for calculation of structural parameter values, graphical methods used to determine position of points and lines, sequence of actions. Analytical record of design development in CAD allows you to repeatedly use once described processes to obtain drawings with other values of parameters. The ability to execute graphical drawings automatically accompanied by their analytical recording greatly accelerates and facilitates the work, but to ensure such a process, each created point and line must be uniquely identified by the system. To do this, it must be given its own name (automatically or by a user). The process record should be available for viewing and editing, descriptions of actions that can't be created in graphic mode (for example, logical ones), as well as for entering necessary comments.

The main conceptual differences in clothing CAD, using analytical recording of processes, is the work on a closed or open scheme.

The ***closed circuit*** means that the descriptions of the processes of calculation and drawing (algorithms) are recorded by the developers in the CAD software, and users set only the values of those parameters that are displayed on the screen.

The ***open circuit*** means that users can write down algorithms on their own, without the help of programmers, in a special language offered by CAD developers to describe graphical and other actions necessary for calculations and construction of drawings of designs and patterns of details of products. Convenience of work under the open scheme depends on quality of the program (simplicity and sufficiency of language of creation of algorithms, convenience of their recording, viewing and editing, synchronism of displaying of carried out actions on the screen, etc.).

Below the peculiarities of performance in different CAD of the main stages of product design are considered.

4. PECULIARITIES OF THE MAIN STAGES OF MODELING AND DESIGN OF SEWING PRODUCTS IN SAPPRE

4.1. Model drawing creation

For development of a design the technical drawing of model on which the product is shown in required proportions, with all design features is necessary.

Drawing can be done in different ways: 1) manually outside CAD; 2) graphically in CAD; 3) analytically in CAD.

In the 90s of the last century in the world there were many graphic systems, with which technical drawings of products are created. Many of them allow you to quickly and accurately perform complex images. However, when developing a design based on a drawing of the model, made manually or in any of the graphic systems, its parameters can be determined only roughly. In the graphic system it is possible to represent also a drawing of product appearance, setting values of parameters at construction. But only the analytical record of drawing creation allows you to turn it into a parametric drawing of the product appearance, in which the model parameters can be directly used in the design development. And when input parameters (measurements of a shape or model features) are changed, such drawing can be automatically rebuilt. If there is a connection between the stages of drawing creation and design development, many parameters (ideally, all of them) are original for the design, and in the already recorded process of model construction, when changing the model parameters, the   drawing should be changed accordingly.

construction. In this case, at the stage of creating a drawing you can work out many parameters of the designed product, specify the range of recommended sizes and growths of the future model.

Creation of a drawing by analytical method in CAD can be done by closed or open scheme.

In the **closed scheme the** surface of a figure (at the three-dimensional image) or its sketches (at the two-dimensional image), and also a kind and constructive divisions of projected clothes "are sewed" by developers in CAD. Therefore only those of them which are displayed on the screen, and within those limits which are established by developers of CAD can be modified.

The **open scheme** allows you to depict any model, any gender and assortment group on a figure of the desired size or without it. If necessary, you can change the surface or sketches of the figure according to its features or build new ones.

4.2. Development of a basic framework in one size

There are four options for obtaining the basic design of the product: 1) **manually** outside the CAD; 2) **graphically in CAD**; 3) **analytically in CAD** by closed circuit; 4) **analytically in CAD** by open circuit.

1.   When developing a basic framework **manually,** geometric information about the parts is entered into CAD using a digitizer, and in some systems - a special scanner.

2.   During the development of the basic design basis in a **graphical way, the** designer, in principle, can work by any method, independently perform the necessary calculations and with the help of graphic operations directly on the screen to build a structure. However, in most cases, it is not rational because of the labor intensity of this process. The system perceives the received points, lines, details as drawing, not bound

neither to the parameters of the figure on which the product is designed, nor to the design parameters. The analogy of its further use can be working with a finished paper base. To obtain a design with other parameters it is necessary either to modify this base

14

by moving contour points and lines, or to perform calculations and drawings anew. Keep in mind that when working in the graphical mode, if the process is not accompanied by its analytical record, it is impossible to change the previously performed actions without destroying the results of subsequent ones.

The development of the structure **by the analytical method** can be carried out **according to the closed** or **open scheme**.

3. If CAD works **according to a closed scheme**, the design procedure is written by the developers in CAD and changes only by them. The user has the possibility to set only the values of the parameters displayed by the developers on the screen. In such systems, only those bases are built automatically and only by the method that is "sewn" in the particular CAD. The result of construction is recorded only for the given model, at its correction or at development of another model it is necessary to repeat the process at first, specifying the parameters again. However, there is still no such a universal design method that would ensure the quality of all construction units for products of different assortment groups and materials of different types satisfying any user without any changes. Therefore, in many cases it is necessary after each new construction of the basis in automatic mode to make the required clarifications in the graphical mode.

4. If CAD works according **to the open scheme**, it is possible to build according to any method, for any kind of products. The user describes the process of calculation and construction of the structure in a special language with the use of variables necessary for calculation, which he calls from the database or sets directly in the process description. The result shall be saved as a program suitable for creating other bases and

model constructions directly or with necessary changes. To obtain a structure with other parameter values it is enough to enter new values, then the recalculation and reconstruction of the structure will be performed automatically.

Work on the open scheme in CAD can be with parallel display of construction on the screen or without it. Designing "blindly", without parallel display of recorded actions on the screen is much more difficult and less obvious than with the display, where you can quickly detect and correct errors. The text of the process description (algorithm) should be saved with the possibility of viewing, editing and copying it.

So that with the help of one program the user could get different variants of construction elements corresponding to certain values of input parameters, CAD should provide description and execution of branching processes. For example, such: "if the total dart solution at the waist is greater than the specified value, two darts are constructed; if less, one dart is constructed".

In addition, significantly accelerate the process of designing new products capabilities:

- allocation of program parts in the form of modules with variable parameters for their use in the development of other basic bases and model structures;
- perform actions on the screen in graphical mode with their automatic analytical record available for viewing and correction;
- recording of cyclic processes, i.e. execution of the program not sequentially but by leaping forward or backward to a specified place under certain conditions. For example: "if the actual value of the pellet landing of the sleeve (Ppossf) is higher than the specified value of X, return to the stage of determining the height of the pellet (Wok), reduce it by the specified value.

the value of Y and repeat the process". The cycle will be repeated until the condition is fulfilled.

4.3. Development of a model structure and a set of moulds in one size

The development of the model design (drawings and patterns of details of a particular model) can also be done by **graphic and analytical methods.**

When graphically transforming a base structure into a model structure, regardless of how the base structure was obtained, it is used as a finished paper base - it can be cut, spread, translate darts, etc. In this case, as already noted, you can not change the previously performed actions without destroying the results of subsequent ones. Therefore, if, after performing a simulation in the graphical mode, the parameters of the basic base built in the analytical mode are corrected, for example, the value of any increase changes, all graphical designs disappear, and they must be performed anew.

In addition, when changing the construction parameter associated with others, it is necessary to make clarifications in the relevant details. This applies both to the main parts (for example, in case of changes in the arm-handle node) and to the derived parts. For example, if as a result of fitting you have changed the neck line, these specifications must be transferred to the back and shelf, to the lining parts (perhaps you can enter the refined details through the digitizer), to build anew the collar or dies.

At an analytical method (work on the closed scheme) only those techniques of modelling and within those limits which are written down in CAD its developers are carried out. For example, if the system provides for the possibility to build relief joints from the shoulder and the armhole, it will not be possible to develop an analytical design with the relief from the neck line.

With the analytic method (work on the open scheme) it is possible to perform any modeling processes, as they are described by the user and saved as programs, which allows to apply them entirely or partially for the development of other models. The length and shape of mating slices of main and derivative parts are maintained according to the description and are automatically changed accordingly when the model parameters are changed.

4.4. Getting moulds in a range of sizes and heights

Model mold sets in the required size and growth range can be built in two ways:
- **gradation of patterns** (technical reproduction);
- **by repeating the process of template building** for other sizes and growths.

In the first case, the patterns of the specified sizes and growths are obtained by modifying the patterns of the base size. The design points on the contour are moved relative to their position in the base size and new contour lines are created, more or less similar to the original ones. To do this operation, the designer must specify for each pattern design point the path of its displacement from size to size and from height to height (called a grading rule or norm), and after the grading system execution, check the length and shape of mating cuttings in each obtained size and, if necessary, correct the norm. Usually, if the model is designed in a wide enough range of sizes to maintain the quality of its fit on the shapes, the grading is done on the size groups, for this purpose, the design for each size group is preliminary developed.

In the second case, when analytical recording of the process of building a base size structure, a set of patterns in a range of sizes and heights
is obtained by automatic repetition of this process by the system for each size of the specified range using the parameters corresponding to the size and growth values. At the same time, the construction accuracy, proportions preservation, conjugation of pattern contour lengths, configuration of lines, and quality of fit of the product in all sizes and growths (if the applied design method allows it) are ensured. Thus, the construction of patterns of different sizes is not only incomparably easier and faster than using grading rules, but also the most accurate method. This is the way, but only by hand, the designers of design methods and grading recommendations determine the displacement of design points from size to size and from height to height. After all, the process of grading (otherwise - technical reproduction of patterns) appeared in the

industrial production of clothing due to the impossibility (due to the extreme labor) of direct construction of drawings of details in the desired range of sizes.

To verify the accuracy of the values of structural parameters obtained by this method in all sizes, the system must be able to automatically determine and print out the values of any structural parameters specified by the user, in all required sizes and growths. In addition, this feature allows you to create in the system and automatically calculate the table of measures (table of measurements of patterns of parts and finished products on given areas for all sizes in which the model should be made).

4.5. Classification of clothing CAD, based on the principles of the stages of construction

Summing up the above, based on the analysis of the principles laid down in the development of software to perform each of the stages of design processes, **CAD clothes can be divided into 4 types**.

CAD of the **first type** as if repeats a part of traditional technology of work of the designer, leaving beyond the limits of automation process of development of primary designs of products. For example, the designer has paper templates, but there is no recorded process of their receipt (methods of construction and specific values of design parameters - additions, coefficients, etc.). These patterns can be modified by methods of structural modeling, for example, to change the position of darts, to enter additional divisions, folds, assemblies, etc. To do it, you may apply model lines on the patterns where they are cut, moved, and then encircle new contours. After you have tried it on, the pattern usually gets refined: it is cut somewhere, added somewhere, the line configuration changes somewhere, and so on. To obtain patterns within the size range, the designer thinks over how the pattern contour nodes should move from size to size and from height to height; he marks these points, draws new contour lines, checks their length, and conjugates corresponding cuts in each size, and specifies position of some points and contour configuration if necessary. Getting patterns for an individual figure may also be done using graphical methods if the designer knows how the design created for it should be changed at existing deviations from the size and shape of the standard figure.

In CAD of the first type, information about manually created patterns is entered into the system through peripheral devices. Modification of the patterns is performed with the help of graphic programs. Getting of patterns in size range is realized by creation (or selection) and assignment of grading rule (norm) to each structural point of pattern contour. After the system carries out the grading, the designer must check the lengths, the configuration of the slice pairing and, if necessary, correct the grading rules and repeat the operation.

In a number of similar CADs to speed up the process of model development, the database contains designs of models of various assortment and polo age groups (as a set of typical dressing). But when developing a particular model, it is often necessary to change some parameters included in the design. For example, to reduce increments to the breast girth or to the armhole depth and width of the sleeve, which can not always be obtained by graphical transformation of the finished base. Thus, in CAD of the first type there is still a large share of manual work, including quite intense and routine - their coefficient of automation is not high enough. The model drawing cannot be created analytically. Therefore, such systems can not serve as a basis for the development of end-to-end design technology.

In CAD of the **second type** for acceleration of reception of base bases with necessary parametres automatic calculation and construction of bases of designs (and sometimes performance of separate elements of constructive modelling) on concrete, sewed up in the program, techniques, i.e. in the analytical way under the closed scheme is provided. In this case, the user can set the values of those parameters, which are displayed by the developer on the screen. Modeling in whole (or in part) is carried out using graphical methods.

The *first significant disadvantage of* this approach is the lack of internal connection between the analytical and graphic stages of model development. The base for graphical drawing is movable, variable (when other parameter values are specified), and the base for graphical drawing is a one-time, unchangeable "superstructure" bound to specific coordinates of points and lines. Therefore, if you need to specify any parameter of the basic construction, e.g., an addition, the system will reconstruct the basic construction, but the entire graphical "superstructure", which is sometimes a significant part of the work, will disappear.

The *second significant drawback of* this approach is the closedness of the system, in particular, the used methods of constructing structures. That is, in such systems it is possible to receive bases only those products, and that way which are provided in the given CAD. For example, if the system laid down only the construction of the foundations of women's clothing by EMCO CMEA, the basis for other methods can not be calculated and built at all. And, as you know, there is no universal methods of design, guaranteeing without any changes to the required quality of landing a variety of products from different materials on the figures with different physiques. In addition, you can not get products of other assortment or gender-aged groups, such as men or children. For these cases, Type 2 systems work as Type 1 CAD.

The *third drawback* is the traditional way to obtain patterns in a size range, i.e. the necessity of a painstaking assignment of grading rules to the design points and all related "pleasures".

Therefore, in some systems **(third type),** try to combine the analytical and graphical approaches in a different way. In these systems, it is possible to write formulas and set variables (X1, X2, etc.) to determine the coordinates of the main structural points. More complex constructions are performed by the user in graphic mode, and the system remembers the performed actions (it records the so-called protocol). If necessary, the values of the variable can be changed and the system reconstructs the drawing. When setting other measurement values for a figure, the construction automatically adjusts according to the process analytical record created and the graphical actions performed. Basically, it is possible to build a basic structure using any method that suits the designer, but it is extremely difficult to design a complex structure with a long construction. For example, if an error is detected in a drawing, or if a graphical operation needs to be performed in a different way (draw a line through another point obtained in the graphical process).

If you want to delete (erase) all graphical constructions that were made after the action to be corrected. Besides, some lines that originally intersected may not intersect in another size or at other values of the variables, points may not get on the line, etc. As a result, the apparent ease of use of analytical and graphic design elements makes real work in the system (building, correction of errors and inaccuracies, making changes after examples, use of previously developed patterns for creation of new models) a laborious and very tense process. It is explained by absence of unequivocal, easily readable and edited record of process.

To the **fourth type it is** possible to carry the systems based on the principle of record deprived of the specified lacks by the designer of all actions which CAD should execute (calculations, introductions of variables, graphic constructions, logic conditions), simple and convenient for the user language with parallel display of construction on the screen. In analytical record for unambiguousness of process each object - a point, a line, a detail, a variable should have the name set by the user or system. At that, quality of implementation of this principle in the system is very important for its convenient use, reliability and speed. There should be: return to any number of steps, editing of the record, copying of the algorithm as a whole or in parts, recording of any comments, creation and calculation of necessary documentation (for example, table of measures, specification and calculation of areas, details' perimeters) and many other things. In case it is necessary to restrict access of others to the calculation and construction methods, there should be an opportunity to close (encode) the text of the algorithm with the password.

The advantage of CAD of the fourth type is not only the creation of a database of ready-made structures, but also the ability to quickly view on the screen all stages of construction and description of the process of development of the structure.
Thanks to this, the designer at any time can use successful solutions in his work, for example, methods of building various structural elements (sleeves, collars of various types, etc.); otherwise, much is forgotten. In addition, continuity is provided when introducing a new designer.

Well-designed CAD of the fourth type, in comparison with all considered types of CAD, provides the maximum coefficient of process automation and allows to solve all mentioned above design tasks. It creates preconditions for development of processes of through designing, allowing to describe construction of the parametrical drawing-drawing of model and its design thanks to what change of parameters of the drawing automatically causes corresponding changes of a design.

5. PRODUCT END-TO-END ENGINEERING

5.1. Development of technology of the through automated designing of clothes

As already noted, one of the most important tasks in the automation of the processes of designing clothes is to ensure communication between the stages of development of the image model and drawings of its design.

The source of information for creating the design of a new model are sketches or technical drawings made by the artist (designer). Technical drawing is more informative for design development than a sketch as it should be performed in real proportions, with all constructive and decorative lines and details. The main requirement for a technical drawing is to get as close as possible to the drawing of the product appearance. Until now, when designing clothes appearance drawings have not been used, because there were no

opportunities for their effective creation. This task can be solved only by computer technologies implemented in CAD, working on an open scheme in the analytical mode. The first industrial system that has such a universal tool for recording and reproducing the processes of calculation and drawing is CAD "Grazia". The author together with L.M. Gladkova and O.V. Zhuravleva developed for the first time the principal scheme and technology of through computer-aided design of products from drawing-drawing of the model to its curves in the range of sizes with all necessary design documentation. This technology was implemented when creating products for women and men's range.

Below are listed the main capabilities of "Grazia" system that allow to carry out end-to-end designing at the stages of drawing and model design development:

1. Write and execute any calculation and construction (without the help of a programmer) in a simple and clear language with the ability to edit the

description and parallel display of construction on the screen.

2. Use of constants and variables required for calculation from databases: general (for example, the values of dimensional features of figures) and related only to the described construction (for example, the list and values of additions to different parts of the construction).

3. Description and execution of branching processes in CAD using the conditional "If" operator.

4. Allocation of any necessary fragments of calculation and construction in modules that can be used in the design of various products, setting the required in each case, the values of parameters.

5. Automatically recalculate and rebuild the drawing at any stage of the process when one or more values change
parameters, as well as in the specified range of sizes and growths at the completion of the description and the drawing development process.

In Grazia CAD, the design process takes place simultaneously on two screen windows - the drawing window and the algorithm window. The process is automatically recorded in the algorithm window. The recording is easy to read, can be corrected at any stage if necessary, and all changes made are immediately reflected in the drawing. The saved algorithm is a program that can also be modified to some extent and saved under a different name. For example, many specific models and other basic algorithms can be created from one basic algorithm. In addition, there are various windows (dimensional features, formulas, etc.) for obtaining information or making changes.

The considered capabilities of Grazia CAD made it possible to implement the task of   ensuring direct communication between stages on its basis.
modeling and design using the algorithm of throughput.
designs. The end-to-end design algorithm contains a description of obtaining a parametric drawing-drawing of the product, product design development and pattern details. At drawing-drawing, numerical parameters of the model to be used at design development are assigned designations and, thus, the status of variables. The design

process is described using these variables. For example, the variables are: base size product length (Dib), base size arm length (Drb), side width (Wb), various additives, etc., which are used to describe the design process. In addition, the parameters may be not only specific values (e.g., height, width, tilt angle) but also configuration of the contour line or division line. Line configuration may be specified by specifying names of start and end points on the line (or on its section) and name of the line itself. The configuration may be changed at the designer's request with the Graphic Correction operator. At that, you may use the "Graphic Correction" operator to change the configuration.

The System automatically records coordinates for playback of the received line.

All parameter values are set interactively by the designer, the result is displayed in the drawing in parallel, it can be specified and corrected at any stage of work.

When you change the value of the parameter, you change the drawing, design, patterns, table of measures. It is more convenient not to assign variable status to some values, and when developing a design, specify that the required value is equal, for example, to the distance (or a certain part of the distance) from the X point to the Y point on the Z line. The system will determine this distance in the figure- drawing as each object (point, line, variable) has its own designation (name). The name unambiguously defines the object because it performs an automatic control that eliminates the possibility of assigning the same names.

The algorithm is also recorded in an interactive mode. For example, you should draw a projection of a point on a line. The user calls the "projection" operation from the "Actions with points" menu. The command line displays a query: "specify a point to be projected". You must use the cursor to specify a point in the drawing and its name appears on the command line. If there is another point in the same place or in close proximity to the specified point, the system will list the names of matching points and ask you which one of them is to be projected. If the designer is not sure of the correct choice, he can easily find a line with a record of the process of obtaining of each of these points and select the desired one (for example, the one obtained by crossing of line X and line Y, and not deferred on line X at a distance of Z). Next, the command line asks: "specify the line we are projecting". After you specify a line, the point you are looking for appears on it, and a new line appears in the algorithm text:

Projection	TN TM LX
Projection	new point old point line

The lower line is a hint describing the structure of the operator record where the cursor is located. Besides, you may get detailed information about any operator by placing the cursor on its name and pressing the F1 key.

Depending on the features of the model in the parametric drawing, it can be depicted in different ways: by itself, worn on a dummy or on a human figure. The developed technology makes it possible to realize all these options. For flat cut products, such as men's and children's shirts, jackets, nursery products, etc. it is convenient to represent the model itself, without the figure. In this case, you can directly specify all the basic design parameters: the length and width of parts in different areas, location, size and configuration of finishing details. Such drawings-drawings with the designation of the measurement points of the product are also convenient for inclusion in the table of measures.

For the development of the model design it may be sufficient to have its drawing in one projection (front view), in two projections (front and rear views), in three projections (front, back, side). You can add a drawing of the inner side of the model, showing where and what pockets are provided, etc.

To depict the model on a dummy or figure, created modules to build sketches of male and female figures (front, rear, side views), as well as dummies. All sketches were built on the basis of measurements (dimensional features) of typical figures (height of anthropometric points, projection and arc measurements, girdles). Materials of the Research Institute of Anthropology of Moscow State University and dimensional standards of standard figures were used. As it is often necessary to set the following for more visualization of the model figure in a certain way, for example, to put aside the hand or leg, were created modules, the input parameters of which are the angles of the hand from the horizontal and leg from the vertical, as well as a module that allows you to bend the hand in the elbow, placing the hand at the waist. Created modules with different hairstyles, as well as modules that allow you to depict a woman's figure in the shoe at the heel, where the height of the heel - a given parameter. Some examples of drawings of sketches of the female figure are shown in Fig. 2.

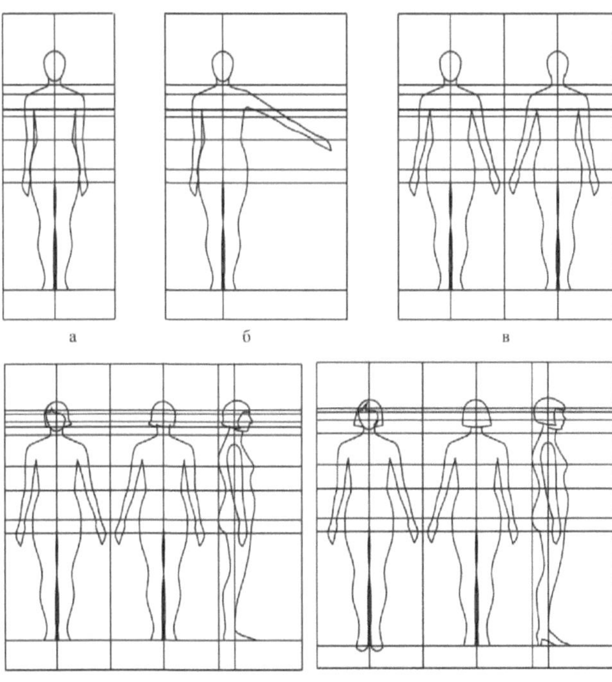

Fig. 2. Sketches of female figures 164-92-100, obtained by execution of modules: a - images of the figure in the face (fas); b - two modules: fas + right hand withdrawal module (ruk); c - four modules: fas + ruk + module of the left hand (rukl) + module of the image of the figure at the back (spina); d - to the option "in" added to the image modules of the figure in the profile (prof) and hairstyle (haier); e - in the option "d" modules fas, prof, haier replaced by modules fasl, profl, haierl

29

5.2. Process of clothes model and design development using
end-to-end design algorithms

The process of model and design development varies depending on whether an end-to-end design algorithm is created for the first time from the very beginning (1), whether a new model is developed using a ready-made algorithm (2), or whether the existing algorithm is modified (3).

1. If you create a end-to-end product design process using the pattern drawing on a figure, the user assigns a name to the algorithm and then performs the following actions.

1.1. Loads the base figure measurement system from the database.

1.2. Calls out from the list the names of modules that play the desired sketches of the figure with the values of input parameters (distances from the edge of the sheet and from each other) and the names of modules position of arms and legs (with the setting of angles). If the resulting figure setting is not satisfactory with something, you can specify the parameters.

1.3. Creates a description of the process of obtaining a drawing of the product with assignment of model variables and their values. Those parameters, which are assigned a symbolic designation (assigned a variable status), are divided into two groups for convenience of work with the algorithm. The first group is entered into the Formulas window. For example, Dib - length of a basic size product, Pg - increase in chest circumference, etc. The second group is written directly into the text of the algorithm in the process of drawing-drawing the model. For example, Vst - the height of the collar stand, Scott - the width of the collar departure, H - the number of buttons, etc. The second group is written directly into the text of the algorithm during the development of the drawing model. In the formula window you can also write down the tabular variables, ie, those whose value depends on the value of one or two other parameters, such as chest circumference, height, silhouette type, etc. The values of all variables can be changed as needed. The division into two groups is quite subjective and can be specified by users. The difference is that the values of the parameters,

You can change the formulas in the formula window at any stage of algorithm execution. In this case, after the command "recalculate", the algorithm is recalculated and executed again from the very beginning, taking into account the corrections made. To change the values of those variables, which are written into the text of the algorithm, you need to place the cursor, indicating the line, up to which the algorithm is executed, not lower than the line, on which the corrected variable is located. The system meets the strict condition that it is impossible to correct the text of the algorithm that has already been executed. Therefore, if you need to change the value of a parameter already specified in the text earlier during the algorithm execution, you should return the cursor to this line and make the necessary corrections. All actions performed with the algorithm are displayed in parallel in the drawing. In the figure. 3 shows the process

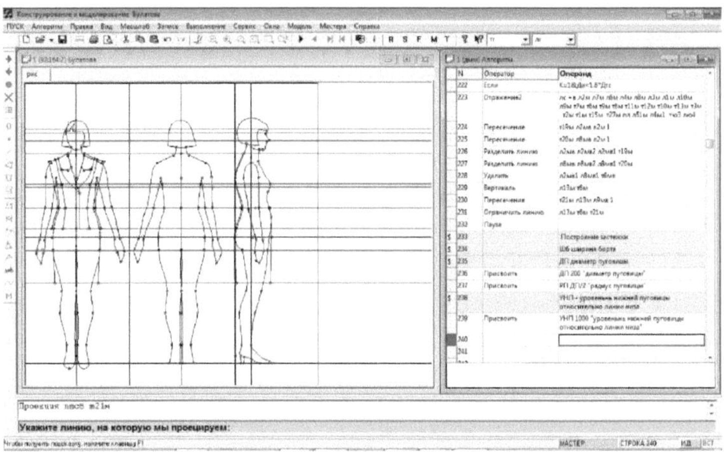

Fig. 3. Development of a drawing of a model of a woman's jacket by analytical method in CAD "Grazia".

creating an algorithm for drawing a model of a female jacket in CAD "Grazia". For convenience, you can increase the image of the drawing to the desired size, call the designations of objects of interest on the screen, as a direct indication of them on the screen, and the operator in the text of the algorithm. In the latter case, all objects participating in the operator execution shall be highlighted (highlighted with color) and their names shall be displayed (fig. 4).

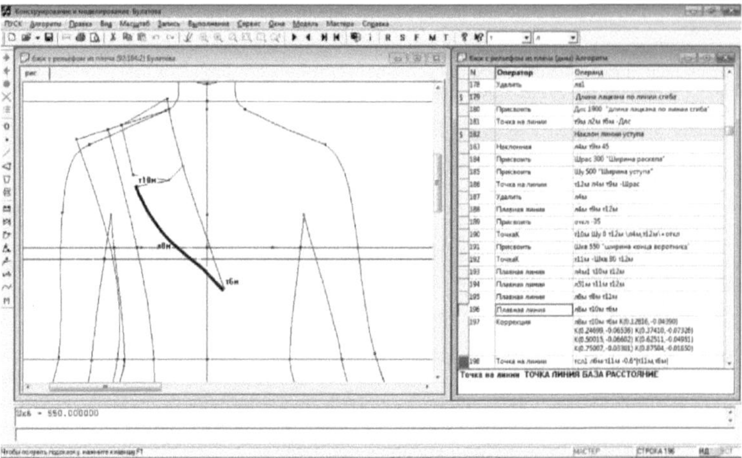

Fig. 4. Show objects participating in execution of the operator specified in the text of the algorithm (marked with a frame)

The parametrical figure-drawing of the model constructed by analytical method at creation of algorithm of through designing is presented in fig. 5.

1.4. The user describes the process of developing a design and patterns of the product using variables assigned when creating a parametric drawing model, and modules of the corresponding stages of construction of the structure (the basis of the mill, darts on the waist line, performing methods of structural modeling, etc.).

Base building modules

mill and sleeve designs were implemented by the All-Union House of Knitwear Models (VDMTI). In order to obtain a structure corresponding to the drawing-drawing of the model created at the previous stage, not only the parameters specified in the form of variables are used, but also directly the product details. For example, in the figure-drawing on the front form are highlighted as an intermediate part of the lapel contour (lapel lapel) and collar[1], as well as the contour of the finishing leaf. Further, when

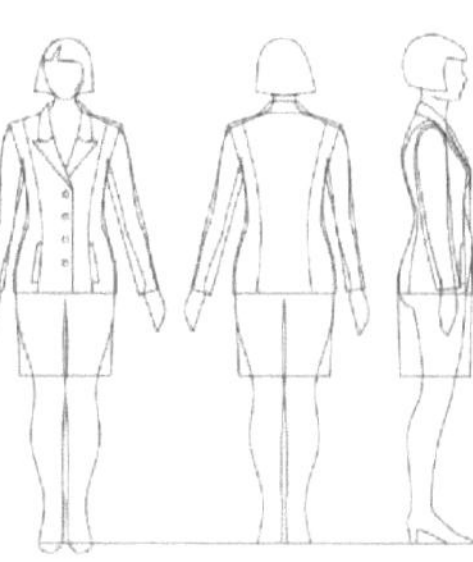

Fig. 5. Picture drawing of women's jacket, created by analytical method using graphical constructions

describing the process of development of the design specifies the place where they are copied (Fig. 6). On this basis, using the values of the height parameters of the rack

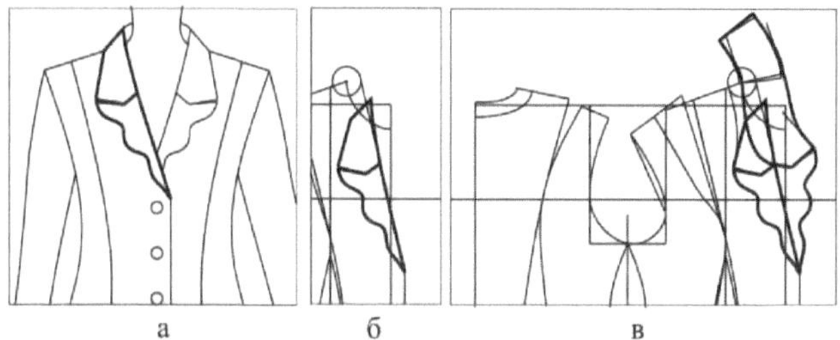

Fig.6. Example of transferring the lapel and the end of the collar from the drawing of the model to the drawing of the structure: a - a fragment of the drawing of the model with a selected intermediate part (bold line); b, c - fragments of a sequential construction drawing of the collar and lapel of the side

---

[1] Error in determining the longitudinal dimensions of the side skirt and the end of the collar in the front form is insignificant, but it is possible to set the exact dimensions, modifying the intermediate piece according to the length taken from the profile projection

(Vst) and the width of departure (Scott), the construction of the collar and turn the board of the product. Construction of collars of various types is allocated to the modules.

For example, developed a module of the jacket collar, which is executed if the Scott <Wst + 1cm (condition, you can .clarify) and the module of the collar blazer type, which is executed if the Scott>Wst + 1cm. Modules are designed with the construction of the tailgate and options for the configuration of the line sharpening (decorated with an angle and rounded). An example drawing of a design constructed during the development of the end-to-end design algorithm is shown in the figure. 7.

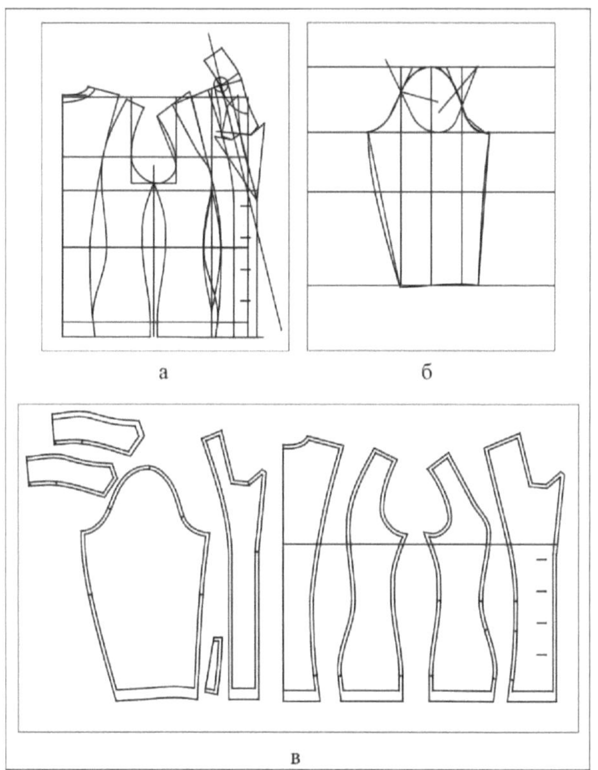

Fig. 7. Drawings of the design and pattern details of the female jacket of knitted fabric: a - the design of the mill; b - the design of the sleeve; c - pattern details.

1.6. The user removes the lines of the body contours under clothing (the operation of deleting unnecessary points and lines is performed to prepare the drawing of the model for export to the graphic program; it completes the text of the algorithm). The drawing - drawing of the product can be sent as a file to any graphic program for development of variants of color and texture solution of the model, creation of necessary inscriptions, printing of the received drawings of the models on printer, storage in an electronic catalog.

Try-drawing of the model   , prepared for export to the graphical program, is given in Fig. 8.

2. If you create a new model of the same cutout as that for which the end-to-end design algorithm is already available, it is enough to save it under the new name (the name of the specific model) and change the values of the initial model parameters. For example, the designer can change the product

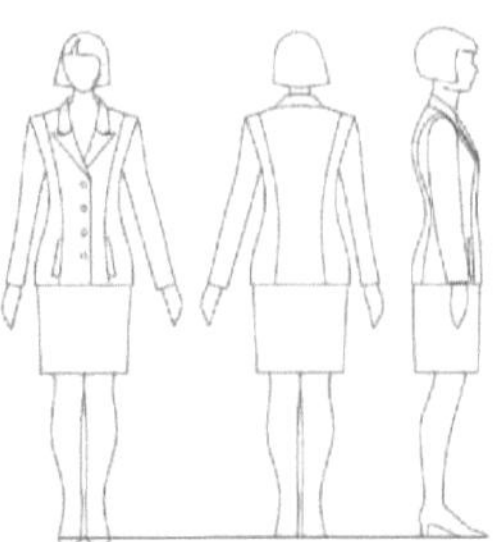

Fig. 8. Picture drawing of the model of the woman's jacket, prepared for export to the graphics program

length, sleeve length, increments at different levels, side width, position and configuration of relief lines, parameters and shape of the collar, lapels, etc. Any change in the value of the parameter in the text of the algorithm or in the "Formula" window is displayed in the figure-drawing. Therefore, the designer can change them, achieving the desired result.

When the system executes this modified algorithm, the design drawings, patterns of main and derivative parts, as well as the table of measures are automatically changed. For example, Fig. 9 shows drawings and moldings of details of several models of women's jackets made of knitted fabric, created by one through design algorithm. The models were developed by the author and students-designers at the practical lessons (Appendix). On the basis of the same algorithm, by varying the values of parameters in the figure, you can obtain images and patterns of an infinite number of models. What they have in common is only the cut (the nature of the division into details): a single sleeve, the back and shelves with reliefs of shoulder seams, collar with lapels. All other characteristics may vary: the silhouette, the position of relief at the shoulder seam and its configuration, side width, the level of inflection of the lapel and the line of dissection, the size and shape of the collar, lapels, the presence and shape of finishing leaves, etc.. And the time spent on the development of patterns of the new model is minimal, depending on the complexity of the cut and usually does not exceed a minute. The main time takes to create a drawing-drawing model - it is a creative part of this process, because the technical side, with a small skill to work with the algorithm is not difficult and requires minimal time. However, when working with the end-to-end design algorithm, you can make any necessary changes in the description of obtaining a sketch-drawing, calculation and construction of the structure, as well as patterns of the model.

In order to work effectively with through algorithms, it is necessary that the design, which is reproduced during the algorithm execution, is well developed for this assortment group and provides a good fit of products of different sizes and heights. It should be noted that there are still quite a lot of uncertainties when designing clothes, which are not subject to full algorithmization, and therefore the model fitting and specification in the material is required. However, to a greater extent, this applies to the development of design in the rest of CAD, when working without a direct link to the drawing-drawing model. In "Grazia" CAD, specifications of the basic design, arising at fitting of a product, are introduced into the algorithm by editing it and saving changes at development of the given model and new models on its basis.

3. If the projected model is different cover (eg, without a collar), you should create a new basic algorithm based on the existing one.

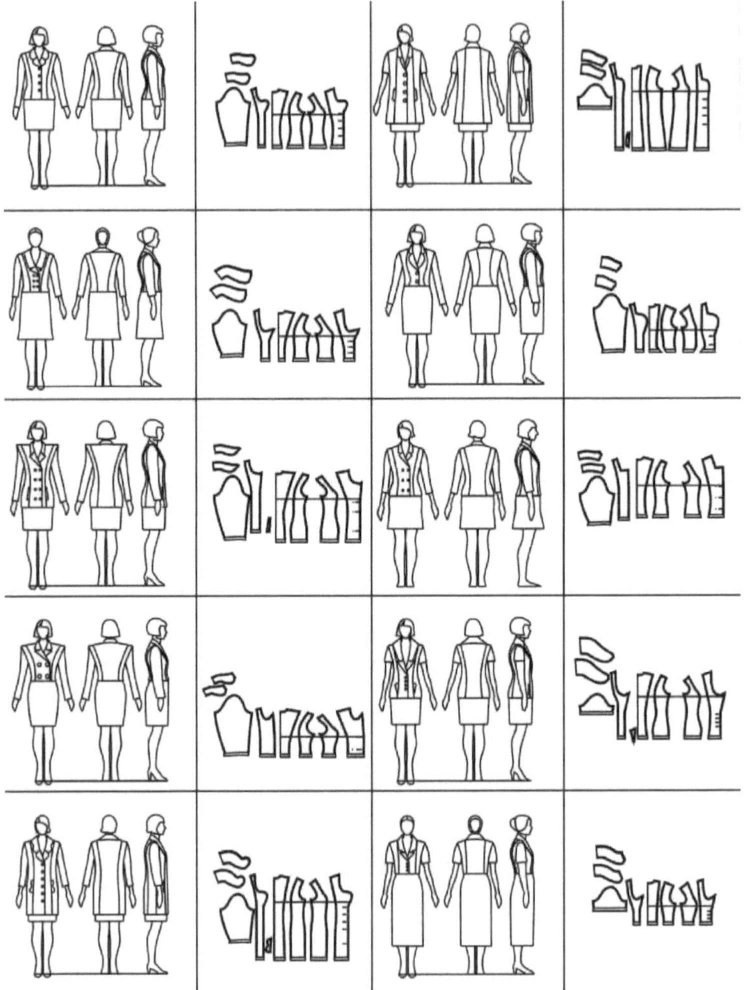

Fig. 9. An example of end-to-end design algorithm usage. Pictures - drawings of models of women's jacket and molded their details, obtained by changing the parameters of the model in the figure-drawing

To do this, save the algorithm under a new name, you need to edit the model drawing and description of the construction. In the example under consideration, in the text of the drawing-drawing you should delete or block[2] those fragments of the algorithm, where the construction of the headboard and collar is set. Then give a description of obtaining the neckline. In the algorithm at the design stage to remove the module to build the collar and further steps with it (the task of allowances for the seams, notches, the grain direction, the multiplicity of parts) and give a description of the construction of the back neckline. In Fig. 10. presents the results of these transformations: figure-drawing model of a woman's jacket without collar, a drawing of the design of his mill, molded details.

If you provide a two-sleeve and reliefs on the back and shelf from the armhole line, you need to specify in the figure-drawing the position of the points of relief beginning, keeping their names, and create modules to build the reliefs from the armhole and getting a two-sleeve. Then adjust the algorithm in accordance with the new process: replace the names of relief modules from the shoulder to the relief from the armhole, single-sleeve to a double-sleeve; make changes to the further description of the construction (highlight the contours of new parts, indicate the location of notches, the number of new parts in the set, etc.).

If the model under development is a suit consisting of a jacket and, for example, a skirt, it is shown in the picture. At that, the parameters necessary for construction of the structure (length of the skirt, additions, etc.) are determined, and the name of the module describing construction of the skirt is written in the text of the algorithm. Model features, which are not taken into account in modules, directly fit into the algorithm, and if they can be used and

---

[2] Grazia" CAD has an option to block any number of algorithm lines. Its essence is that when the algorithm is executed, the system skips the locked lines. This makes it possible not to remove them from the text of the algorithm. In addition, the locked lines can be explained and any necessary entries can be made on the line marked with a sign. Locked lines are automatically highlighted in color.

still in some models - are made out as a new module. New modules can be created "from scratch" or be obtained by copying and editing existing ones.

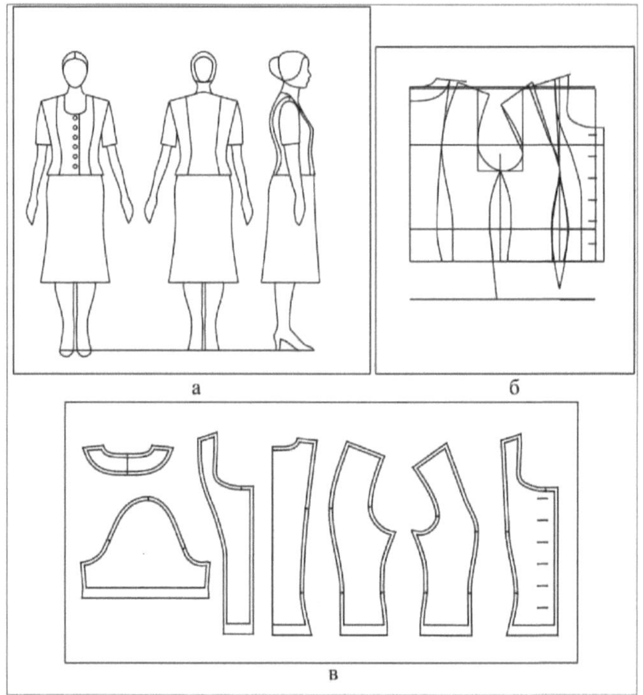

Fig. 10. Drawing-drawing of a female jacket without collar, the design of the mill and molded the details of the jacket, developed on the basis of the algorithm of through design of a female jacket with a collar.

To build a design, not all parameters can be directly taken from the drawing of the product depicted on the figure or dummy, as the dimensions in width in the drawing are distorted.

But it does not mean that you need to build horizontal sections or three-dimensional images to define such sizes.

Currently, there is not enough information on how to take into account the properties of the material in the transition from a given three-dimensional surface of the product to its deployment. But experienced designers even on the technical drawing can determine with sufficient accuracy the values of the necessary additives to girth measurements for the materials with which they work. Therefore, when working with a drawing of the product, which shows the outlines of the figure, can not cause additional problems. In addition, there is an option to formalize the accumulated experience in the database. For example, it is possible to create tables of additions values for different silhouette solutions by types of materials or coefficients to obtain the width of the product at the appropriate levels on the shape shown in the face in the profile. The silhouette solution can be defined, for example, by specific values of gaps between the contours of clothing and body at the level for which the allowance is defined.

Picture drawing of the model presented in three projections is sufficient to determine the position and configuration of the model lines in the design, even if the line itself is visible in the picture with distortion. It is necessary to find the parameter (or a number of parameters) by means of which it is possible to receive the set line in the design drawing. For example, when developing an algorithm for end-to-end design of a jacket with reliefs from the armhole line or with raglan sleeves (Fig. 11) defines their configuration in the front and back. After that the length from the relief start points on the back and shelf along the armhole line to the end of the shoulder seam (or to notches on the armhole line) is taken as a parameter on the profile projection.

Description of template development process in the through algorithm can also be specified. For example, the values of allowances for seams, the design of corners of parts with allowances. The basic algorithm gives values typical for the type of material on which the algorithm was developed. But these parameters are 40 depend on a number of reasons (joint design, material properties, technology adopted at the enterprise). Recording of the operation of seam allowance construction in the "Seam" operator is easily corrected if necessary. It is possible to change values of allowance for seams, design of angular sections of cuts. The Grazia System allows to specify 25 variants of cut corners design, the major part of which was identified and formalized by O. V. Surikova[3]. When the Seam operator is executed, the type of corner design selected from the table (with a description and a schematic drawing) is written into the operator's record line after the name of the corresponding point on the pattern

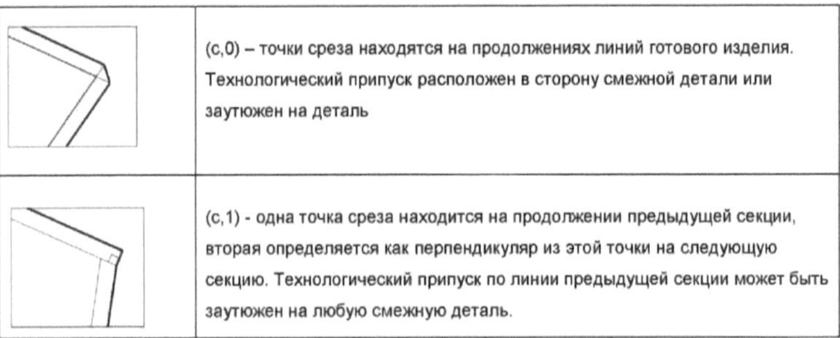

	(с,0) – точки среза находятся на продолжениях линий готового изделия. Технологический припуск расположен в сторону смежной детали или заутюжен на деталь
	(с,1) - одна точка среза находится на продолжении предыдущей секции, вторая определяется как перпендикуляр из этой точки на следующую секцию. Технологический припуск по линии предыдущей секции может быть заутюжен на любую смежную деталь.

contour. For example:

It should be noted that the creation of algorithms for the through design of new cuts of clothing is quite time-consuming, requires certain skills and thorough testing of the correctness of their performance at various values of parameters. However, the result repeatedly reduces labor costs for the development of new models and allows you to create almost unlimited number of models with ready-made design documentation for further selection.

---

[3]Surikova O.V. "Design of rational designs of clothes details on the basis of computer technologies", dissertation for the degree of Candidate of Technical Sciences. Ivanovo State Textile Academy, 2004.

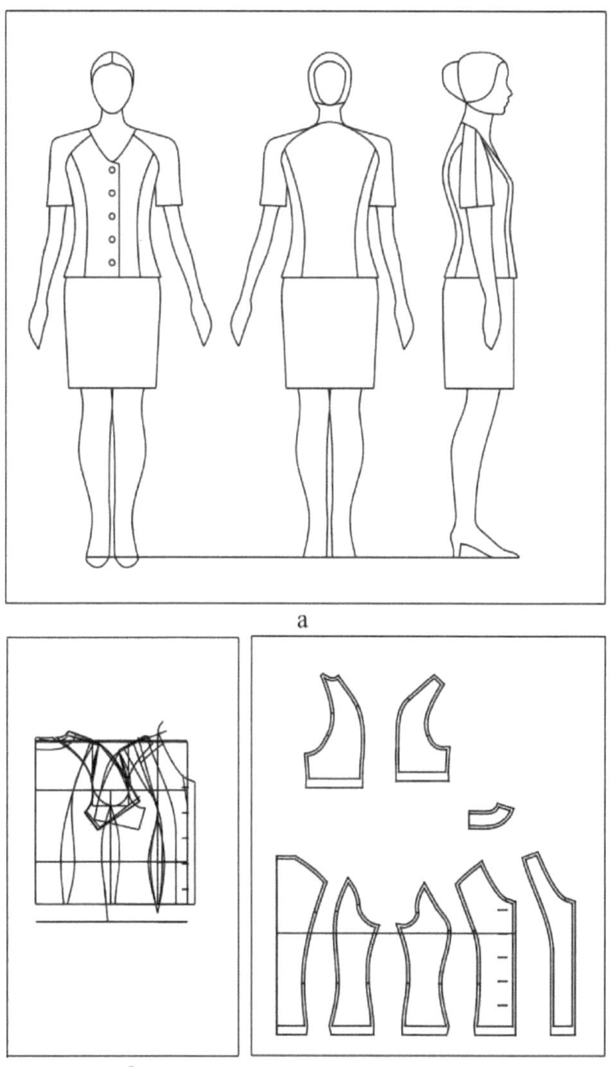

Figure 11: Drawing of a female raglan-cut jacket (a), its design (b) and details (c), created by the algorithm of through design

5.3. Determination of the recommended size range for the projected model and the possibility of expanding it by harmonizing the proportions.

Another very significant advantage of end-to-end design is that it allows at the stage of model drawing development not only to work it out on the figure of base size and height, but also to see how the model will look on figures of other sizes and heights. For this purpose, it is enough to specify the required size, height, and completeness as a basic variant and the system will quickly automatically rebuild the drawing. The example is shown in fig. 12.

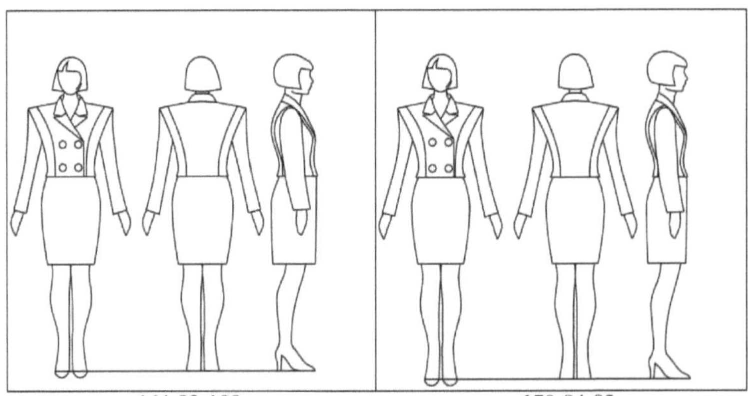

Fig. 12. Figure- drawing of a model of a woman's jacket on figures of different sizes.

As a result, you can reasonably determine the size and growth range in which the model looks good. In addition, there is a unique opportunity to expand the range of sizes by refining the proportions of designed products in different sizes and heights. For example, a suit designed for a figure 164-92-100 (fig. 13) looks bad on high.

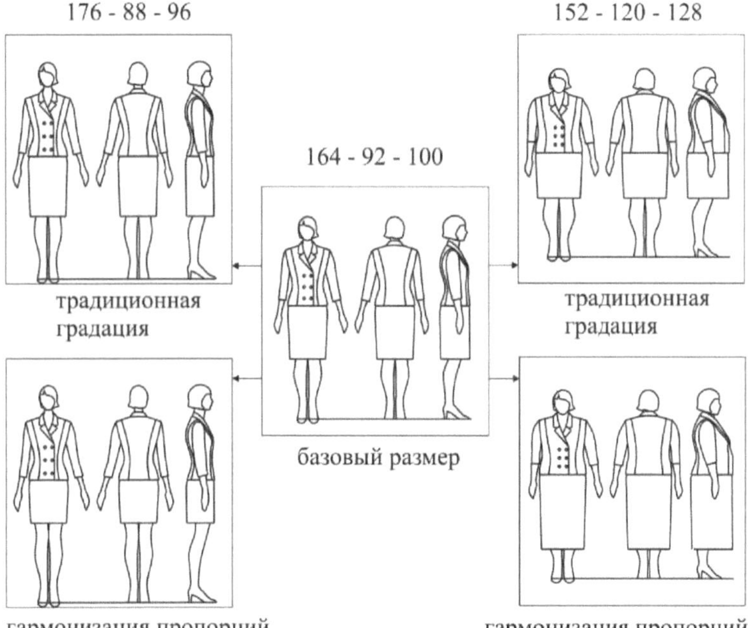

Figure 13: A model worked out in a base size (164-92-100), on shapes of other sizes and sizes in traditional grading (in proportions of the base size) and after harmonization of proportions.

skinny and low full women. But it can also be produced in these sizes, if you change the length of the skirt in a different way than it is usual at present (with retaining the proportions along the length of the base size, without taking into account the change in the width of the shape). For this purpose, you should review the model drawing in different sizes and heights and harmonize proportions by choosing the necessary parameters values (in the example under consideration - skirt length). The length found for each size and height shall be entered into the database table of the model. The System shall automatically build the patterns of the corresponding length and enter their parameters into the Table of Measures. The illustration shows the simplest example for illustrative purposes. But it does not exhaust the possibilities of harmonization of proportions in the end-to-end design. Similarly, it is possible to specify other design parameters of the product, most suitable for figures of different sizes and growths.

As it has been already mentioned, the analytical description of the process of development of the structure and model patterns eliminates the need for gradation of patterns. Molds in a given range of sizes and growths are created by the system automatically by repeating the algorithm execution with values of dimensional attributes and other parameters corresponding to standard figures, for which the model is designed. The patterns may be rebuilt also for an individual figure at input of its measurement values.

Cross-cutting design allows you to quickly calculate all the main technical and economic indicators before making a model sample and more reasonably assess the expediency of its launch into production, because after creating the appearance of the model in the drawing-drawing of its patterns are built automatically, and from them in the system can quickly make a layout and perform other design procedures.

Despite the fact that CAD "Grazia" for many years has been successfully used in the design of various types of clothing at many large and small enterprises, model houses and ateliers, the through design of clothing models, unfortunately, is not yet used in production.

This is partly due to a certain complexity and labor intensity of writing a through algorithm, which is difficult to implement in the conditions of the current production, if necessary, to obtain a rapid result. As initially spent efforts in the future repeatedly will be justified, more real is performance of this work by order of external executors for concrete assortment groups of products of necessary coverings in direct contact to designers of the enterprise.

5.4. Cross-cutting accessory design (headgear, handbags)

For the design of a number of products, such as hats and bags, through algorithms can already be effectively used at enterprises, as the design of such products is not difficult to create drawings of their appearance in real size.

At designing bags working projections of created products are used[4] for a long time, on their basis patterns of details are developed.

As for the models of sewn headwear of new forms, their development was quite labor-intensive in traditional ways. Therefore most often the enterprises let out a collection of the models created on the basis of several forms, worked out by a breadboard model way. For the modeling usually use pre-designed rigid forms of the inner surface of the future headgear. A variety of models is achieved through the use of different materials and finishes. Sometimes decorative divisions of parts are introduced.

In this connection, in order to obtain the headgear designs of any shape conceived by the designer, the author has developed a technique of modeling and design of headgear by engineering methods. The technique provides for the creation of vertical and horizontal projections of the supporting surface of a person's head, the construction of their sections and sweeps of parts on which the surface is divided by structural and decorative lines. This technique has been taught for a number of years to design students in the Russian State University of Technical University and Technology, to manufacturers (designers and designers of headwear) - at seminars, as well as presented in a book[5] and in journal publications.

---

[4] Design of products from leather / Zybin Yul., Klyuchnikova V.M., Kochetkova S.S., Fukin V.A., - M.: Light and Food Industry 1982. - 382c.

[5] Bulatova E.B. Modeling and design of headdresses. Textbook for HEIs. / E.B. Bulatova.- M., Academy, 2007. - 112c.

Thus, even in case of manual design of headgear and bags, through algorithms are already used, where the initial data for design development are directly taken from the model appearance drawing. The automation of these processes is therefore much simpler. According to the method of modeling and designing of headdresses by projections and sections, basic algorithms of through designing of different types of headdresses have been developed. According to the section configuration on the level of head circumference the headdresses can be divided into "round" (section - circle) and "oval" (section approaching to oval). To "round" hats are berets, many women's hats, men's caps and hats earflaps, to "oval" - most men's hats and caps.

Many "round" headdresses are rotation surfaces and therefore two projections - vertical and horizontal - are enough to construct their sweeps (Fig. 14). If the product surface is not a surface rotation, you should specify at least three projections - the front, side and top views (Fig. 15).

High accuracy is required when drawing parts and manufacturing headgear, as small deviations in the size of parts have a significant impact on the size and shape of the finished product. For example, the error in determining the width of half a symmetrical wedge by 1 mm in a classic beret consisting of 8 wedges (see Fig. 14) will be equal: 1*2*8=16 mm, i.e. more than one and a half sizes. In addition, the change

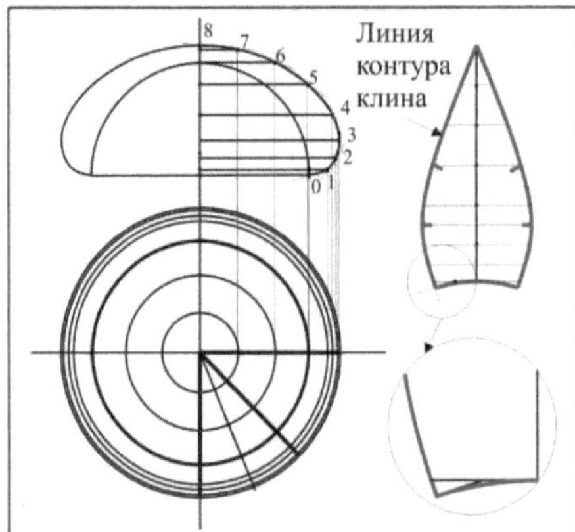

Fig. 14: Designing a beret of 8 wedges by
projections and cross sections

the thickness of the bundle of materials from which the headgear will be made also leads to a change in the size of the finished product.

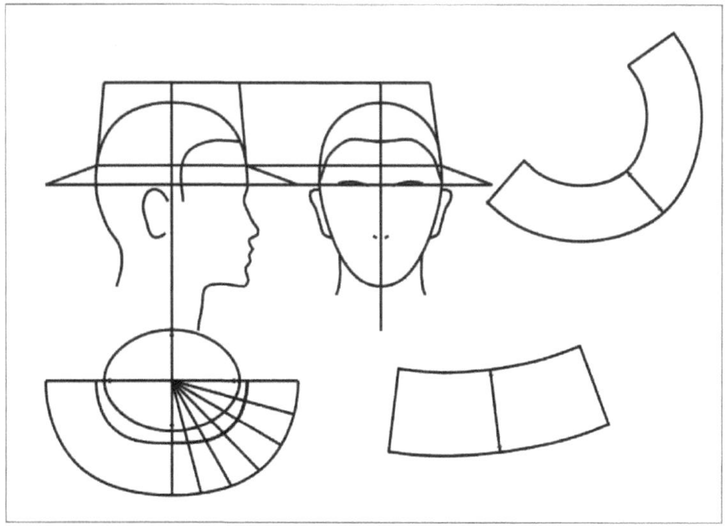
Fig. 15. Design of a hat with fields

The end-to-end design algorithms allow to obtain with high accuracy the patterns of the models created by the designer within the specified in the algorithm cut (Fig. 16,a), and can also serve as a basis for the development of various models with changes in cut (Fig. 16,b-d).

In this case, the library of basic end-to-end algorithms increases.
Cross-cutting design opens up a wide range of possibilities for creating hats with complex fantasy division, providing high precision patterns across the entire size range, which is almost impossible to achieve with manual design. Especially promising is the creation of models with division into small parts for products made of expensive materials, such as fur. Memberships make it possible to create interesting ones,

unusual models that can use even small pieces that usually go into waste (Figures 17,18).

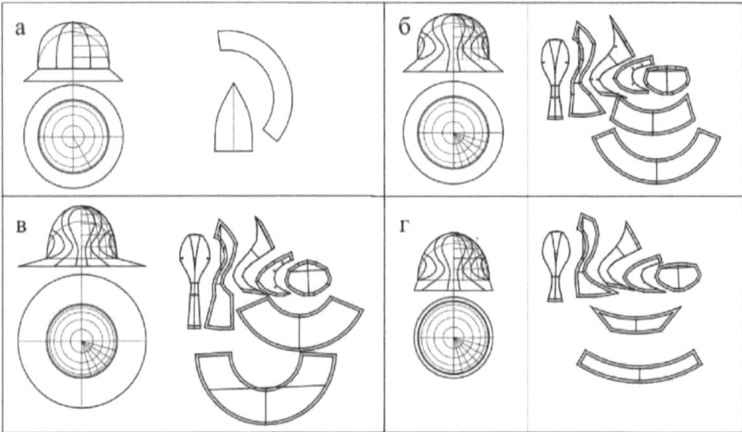

Fig. 16. Projections and design of a flat, obtained from the basic algorithm (a); fantasy division model, created from the basic algorithm (b); female flat models, obtained from the fantasy division algorithm (c, d).

The program allows you to save graphic information from "Grazia" in HPGL and BMP formats, so the files are exported as vector or raster images in graphic programs, for example, in Corel Draw and Adobe Photoshop, where you can work through the color solutions of models and present them visually before manufacturing (see Fig. 18).

There are two possible approaches to creating basic algorithms of end-to-end design.

The first is the development of *a family of basic algorithms* with some differences in the cut or design process.

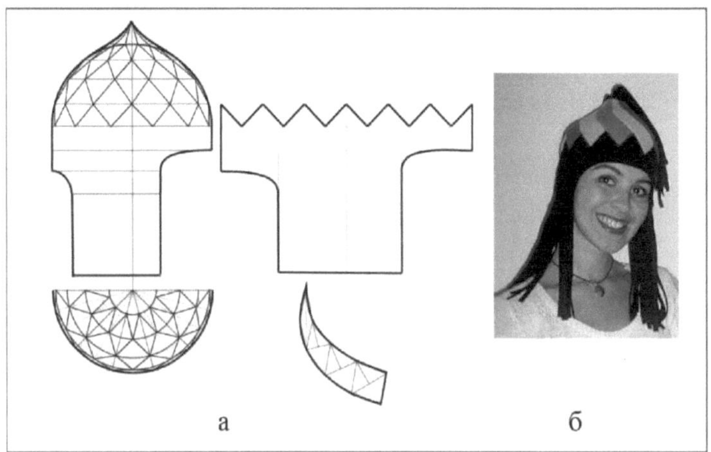

Fig. 17: Model and design development of the headgear by projections and sections (a) and photography of the finished product (b)

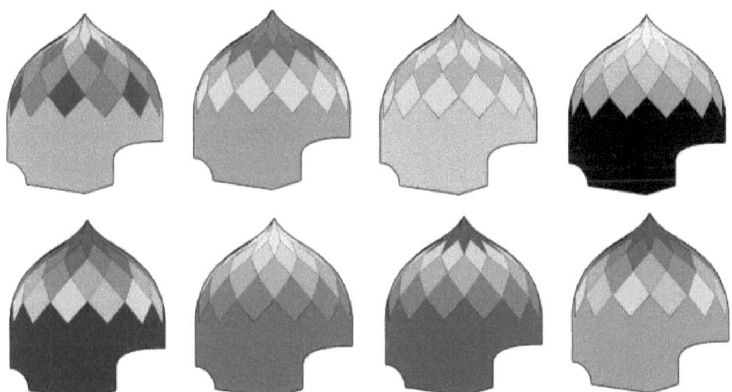

Fig. 18. Development of color variants of the headgear model

The second is the creation of a *universal basic algorithm that* covers this family. For example, for the design of a hat with fields, the body of which consists of a wall and a trough, originally developed several basic algorithms. The basic (classical variant) - with a horizontal trough and field edge, as well as the algorithms created on its basis: with a sloping trough, with a curved trough, with a sloping line of field edge, and others.

Currently, a universal basic algorithm has been developed, which includes all these options. Universality is achieved due to the possibility to describe branching processes in CAD "Grazia" using the "if" operator.

Fig. 19 shows some hat models obtained by changing parameters of the universal algorithm. Opening the formula window (Table 1), the designer sets the variants of troughs, fields and saves the algorithm under the name of the new model.

Variant in=0,   n=0 (classic) is automatically executed in all cases. In this case, in accordance with the artistic plan, in the process of working out the drawing-drawing of the model in the initial basic algorithm, you can change the level of the additive line [6]relative to the level of measurement of head circumference, height of the torso, angles of inclination of the torso and fields in front, back and side, width of the fields, configuration of the bottom. The system then performs a fragment of the algorithm corresponding to the specified condition, ignoring all other possible options. For example, in case of the variant in=2, n=1, the system skips the algorithm fragments with the construction description in=1, n=0; in=1, n=1; in=2, n=0, executing only the sequence of actions enclosed in brackets and the next one after the indication "if in=2&n=1".

---

[6] Additive - the line of articulation of the torso with the fields, and in the absence of fields - the line of the lower edge of the headdress.

Table 1

Formulas

№	Name	Designation	Formula	Meaning
15	Height (thickness) of the material (bag) taking into account kneadability,	Wms	0	0
16	Thickness allowance of material (bag of materials) to the half girth of the head	Pt	3.14*BMS	0
17	Variant bottom. The bottom is parallel to the base, in=0. If the bottom is not parallel to the base, you can specify a variant: in = 1 - the bottom lies in an inclined plane, in = 2 - the line of the middle of the bottom - a smooth curve (up to half straight, the second half - a smooth curve), in = 3 - the line of the middle of the bottom - a smooth convex curve, in = 4 - sloping bottom with a fold or a seam in the middle line, the upper edges of the wall in the form of side - convex curves; c=5 - line of the bottom middle - a smooth convex curve; c=6 - line of the bottom middle - a smooth curve (to the middle of a straight line, the second half - a smooth curve, transitioning into a band on the torso); c=7 - line of the bottom middle - a smooth convex curve, back and front, transitioning into strips on the torso	B	1	1
18	Variant fields. If the margin of the fields is horizontal - n=0; if it is sloped - n=1.	п	0	0

When developing a new model (Fig. 20), the designer, having specified any variants of the trough and margins, may not change the values of other parameters of the base algorithm (Fig. 20,a), then the construction will be executed in a few seconds. But he may refine them by changing the position of the point determining the bending

53

beginning of the tulle profile contour and its configuration (Fig. 20,b,c,d).

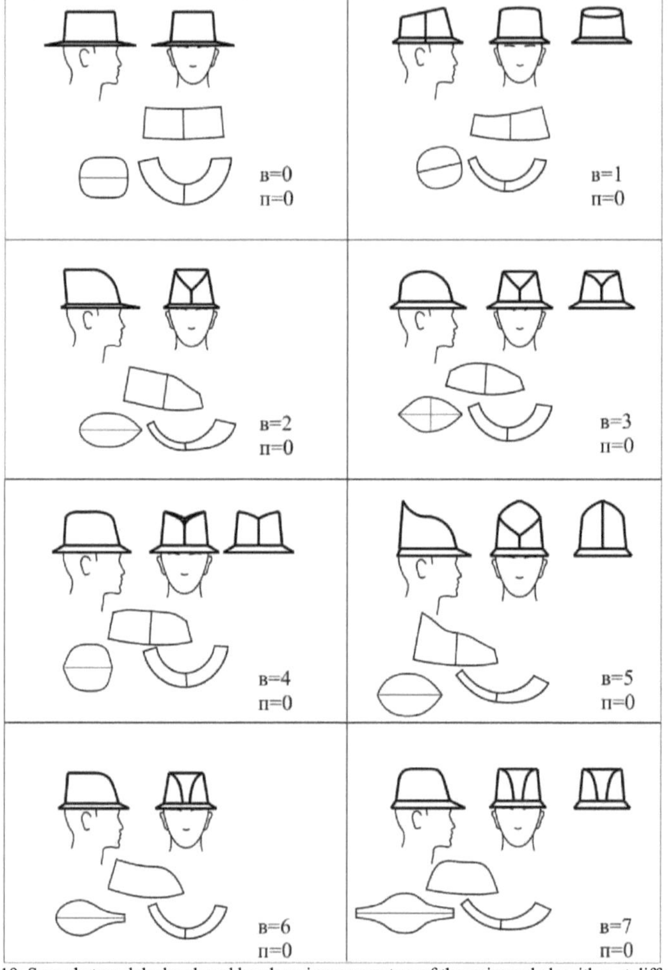

Fig. 19. Some hat models developed by changing parameters of the universal algorithm at different values of the bottom (c) and the same (horizontal) edge of the fields (n=0).

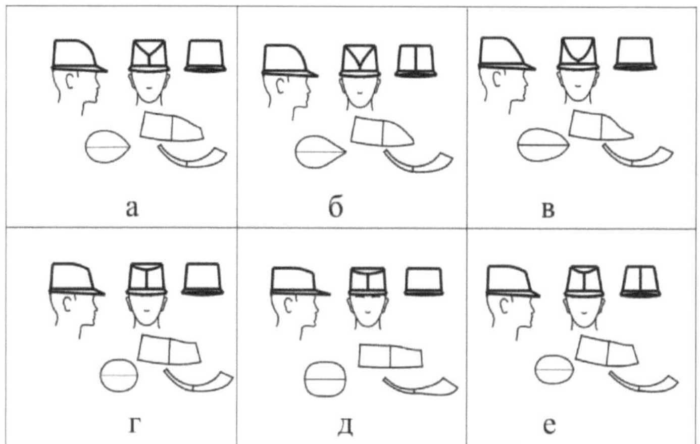

Fig. 20. Examples of creating new models with constant values of parameters determining the variant of the bottom (in=2) and the edges of the fields (n=1).

If you need to improve the obtained model, you can change the values of previously set parameters: inclination angles, torso height, etc. (fig. 20,e,f). The time of algorithm execution (getting the product details) is increased for the time of its artwork (defining the required parameter values). To obtain patterns for a particular model, you need to enter the thickness of the material package along the additive line (Bms), specify the number and position of joints in the patterns (it is supposed to bend or stitch), set the seam allowance[7], notches and direction of grain lines, specify the number of patterns of each type in the model, and assign a class to the patterns (possibility of their location in one layout). The system executes

---

[7] In the basic and universal algorithms of headgear design it makes no sense to add seam allowance to the contours of parts, because depending on the materials used (fur, leather, fabric, knitwear) is chosen the design of the seam and the value of the allowance for the seam. In symmetrical parts, a bend or a seam can be designed. Therefore it is advisable to set the seam allowance already when developing a specific model based on a basic algorithm.

construction of patterns in the required size range, creates a specification of details, calculates their areas.

On the basis of the universal algorithm it is possible to develop models with different cut, for example, instead of fields to provide a visor. For this purpose, the part of the algorithm describing the construction of fields is blocked and the visor module of the required type is called. The module also provides for varying the values of parameters that determine the appearance of the visor: slope angle, width, etc. In the new models, you can enter additional divisions, such as the dotted bezel, as well as change the details by methods of constructive modeling, creating, for example, draperies or folds on the body. Successful solutions themselves become basic algorithms for creating new models or complement the universal algorithm.

The big advantage of end-to-end headgear design is that, having developed model patterns in the base size, it is only necessary to set the size range, and the system will automatically rebuild patterns to all sizes of the range (Fig. 21). At present, with other methods of model and design development, especially with unconventional shape or division of the product, it is very difficult to obtain moldings of other sizes while maintaining the similarity of the base size model.

In addition, when using end-to-end design algorithms, the model can be initially executed from the layout material, if necessary, to clarify any parameters and make these changes to the text of the algorithm. Then, you should enter the values of material package thickness in the support area (taking into account the seam construction and material thickness) - the patterns will also be rebuilt automatically. This is important, because if the thickness of the material packet is not taken into account, the inner perimeter of the headgear along the head circumference line will be reduced by 1.9 cm, i.e. practically by 2 sizes at its magnification by 3 mm. To control in universal algorithms, the parameters of external and internal perimeters of the headgear have been introduced in the table of measures.

support area (Table 2). In the above example, the thickness of the material package is set to 5 mm.

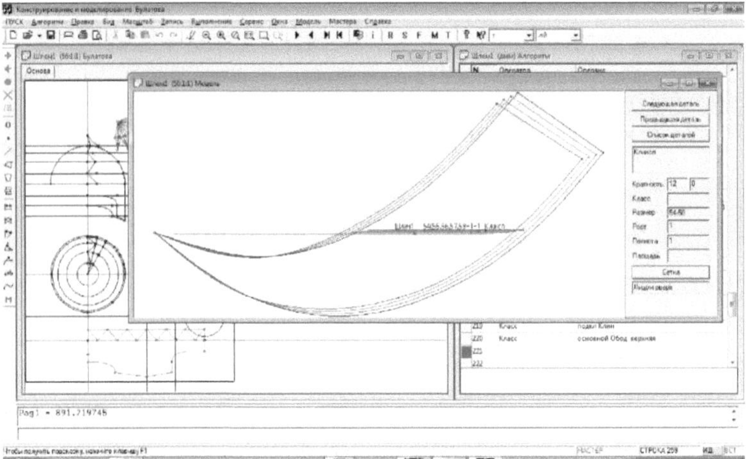

Fig.21. Viewing the pattern grid in the "Models" window

Table 2

Part of the report card of the headgear measures

Name	Size							
	53	54	55	56	57	58	59	60	61
Product perimeter in the bearing area internal	53.0	54.0	55.0	56.0	57.0	58.0	59.0	60.0	61.0
Product perimeter in the bearing area external	56.2	57.2	58.2	59.2	60.2	61.2	62.2	63.2	64.2

The use of universal end-to-end design algorithms in "Grazia" CAD allows for incomparably faster development of the required number of new various models than with any other design method.

The same applies to the bags. Fig. 22 shows a drawing of model and design of the bag created by projections and sections. On fig. 23

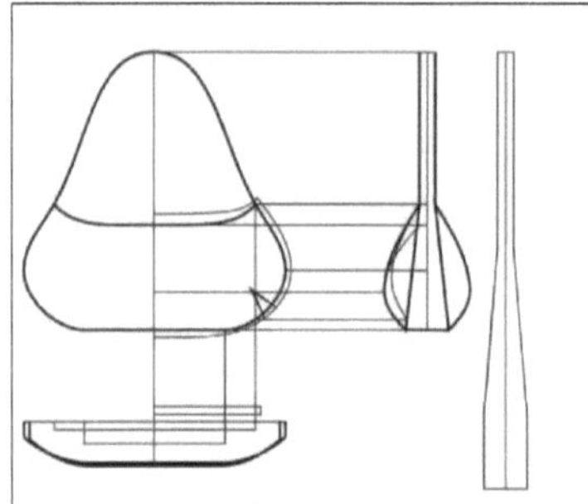

Fig.22. Designing a bag by
projections and cross-sections

shows the sketch of the bag and some variants of the same cut, obtained only by changing the contours of the product on the front and side views. This possibility of changing the appearance of the product using this algorithm is not exhaustive. You can change the length and width of the handle, the width of the nerd[8] in different

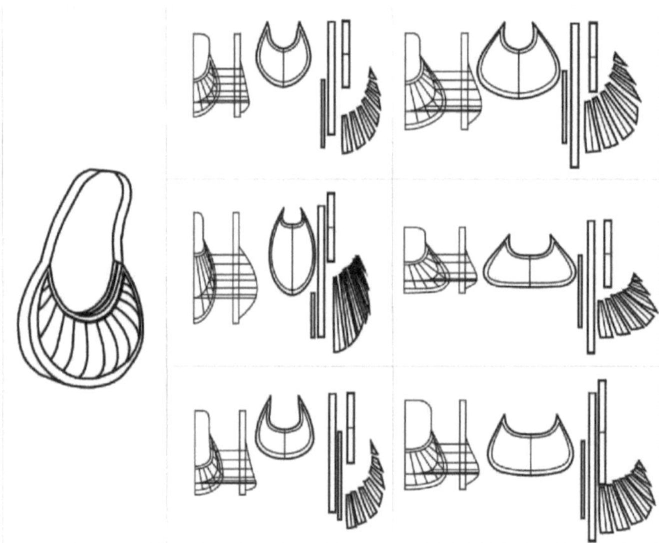

areas.

Fig. 23. The sketch of the bag, projections and model patterns obtained by one basic algorithm developed in accordance with the presented sketch.

When you make corrections to the algorithm, you can change the configuration

---

Nerd (top, bottom) - part that forms the side and top and/or bottom surfaces of the bag case.

and number of bag pocket members, enter additional members, transform the pocket into the bag wall, etc.

Throughput computer-aided design of headgear and bags provides high accuracy of obtained patterns and is carried out many times faster than in the widely used nowadays layout method.

In addition, there is an automatic calculation of areas of patterns, drawing up a specification of details.

When connecting other subsystems ("Manufacturing Technology", "Layout", "Dispatching", "Accounting and Planning", "Business Management"), the execution of end-to-end algorithms in the subsystem "Design and Modeling" can be a stage of complex automation offered by CAD "Grazia". All this will not only significantly reduce labor costs in the design and preparation for the production of new models, but also reduce their material intensity, as well as optimize the planning and production cycle of products.

In conclusion, I would like to emphasize once again that the end-to-end design of products reveals huge, previously unavailable opportunities for development and preparation for the launch of new models, and it is waiting for its enthusiasts.

PERFORMANCE VALIDATION

The developed computer technologies of end-to-end design of clothes and accessories have been tested both in the training process and in production. They were demonstrated at Federal Wholesale Fairs of goods and equipment of textile and light industry, at other exhibitions and fairs, marked with diplomas and certificates. The author was awarded two gold medals of the All-Russian Exhibition Center (VVC) for the development of the technology of through computer-aided design of clothes and headwear. Repeatedly there were held school-seminars and master classes at the enterprises, in the Model Houses, educational institutions, and also at the exhibitions-fairs.

The results are presented in training manuals and publications.

1. *Bulatova E.B. The* new approach to automation of designing of clothes / E.B. Bulatova, E.B. Koblyakova, N.K. Voropaeva // Sewing industry - [1] 2 - 1999

2. *Bulatova E.B.* Computer technologies of designing of clothes on the basis of system "Grazia" / E. B. Bulatova, V. G. Eschenko, V. V. Razmakhnina // Sewing industry - [1] 1 - 2000

3. *Bulatova E.B.* New opportunities for improvement of design processes provided by CAD "Grazia" / E.B. Bulatova, L.M. Gladkova, O.V. Zhuravleva // Sewing industry - [1] 4 - 2000

4. *Bulatova E.B.* Through Modular Design of Products in CAD "Grazia" / E. B. Bulatova, L. M. Gladkova, O. V. Zhuravleva // Sewing Industry - № 5 - 2001

5. *Bulatova E.B.* Why "Grazia"? / E.B. Bulatova, V.G. Eschenko // World of equipment - [1] 3 - 2002

6. *Bulatova E.B.* Constructive Modeling of Clothing: a Textbook for Universities / E. B. Bulatova, M. N. Evseeva - M.: Academy - 2003

7. *Bulatova E.B.* CAD Evaluation Criteria: Abstracts / E. B. Bulatova // Proceedings of the scientific and methodological conference "Education in the field of service in the era of globalization: problems, prospects for development". - M: MGUS - 2004

8. *Bulatova E.B.* Implementation of cyclic processes in the design of clothes in CAD

"Grazia": thesis / E. B. Bulatova, O. Zhuravleva. V. // Proceedings of scientific and methodical conference "Education in the service sphere in the era of globalization: problems, prospects of development". - M: MGUS - 2004

9. *Bulatova E.B.* Design of headgear by projections and sections: theses / E. B. Bulatova // Proceedings of scientific and methodical conference "Education in the field of service in the era of globalization: problems, prospects for development". - M: MGUS - 2004

10. *B. G. Eschenko* Increase of competitiveness of sewing enterprises on the basis of high technologies / V. G. Eschenko, E. B. Bulatova // In the world of equipment - [1] 2 - 2005

11. *Bulatova E.B.* CAD Evaluation Criteria / E. B. Bulatova // Garment Industry - № 8 - 2005

12. *Bulatova E.B.* Approaches to the choice of CAD: who is warned is armed / E. B. Bulatova, G. I. Surikova, V. G. Eschenko, V. V. Svetikov // In the world of equipment - № 4 - 2005

13. *Bulatova E.B.* Author's Methodology of Teaching Headgear Design: Abstracts / E. B. Bulatova // Proceedings of the Scientific and Methodical Conference - M.: MSUE - 2006.

14. *Bulatova E.B.* Modeling and design of headgear: a textbook for higher educational institutions. / E.B. Bulatova - M.: Academy, 2007

15. *Bulatova, E.B.* If to automate designing / E.B. Bulatova. // Headdresses and accessories - [1]4 - 2008

16. *Bulatova E.B.* New technique of modeling and designing of headgear and its implementation in CAD "Grazia" / E.B. Bulatova // Clothing industry - [1]5 - 2008

17. *Bulatova E.B.* Through Automated Design of Products in CAD "Grazia" - the solution of the problem of communication between the stages of modeling and design / Bulatova E. B. / / / Clothing Industry - [1] 4 - 2010

18. *Bulatova E.B.* Lessons of headgear design from Bulatova E.B. / E.B. Bulatova // Headgear. Templates, design, technologies - issue № 6 - 2010

19. *Bulatova E.B.* Designing headwear in CAD "Grazia" with the help of universal

algorithms / E. B. Bulatova // Sewing industry - ¹ 4 - 2011

PRACTICAL WORKS IN THE DISCIPLINE "COMPUTER ENGINEERING IN FASHION DESIGN"

Subject: development of models of women's jackets and technical documentation based on the algorithms of through design in CAD "Grazia".

Purpose of work: mastering of methods and practical methods of development of new models and technical documentation based on the use of algorithms of through design in CAD "Grazia".

Assignment

1. Study possibilities of creating a new model based on the model of the same cover by changing parameters of line construction and configuration in the parametrical drawing:

- length of skirt, jacket, sleeves;

- silhouette (addition along the lines of the chest, waist, hips; to the depth of the armhole, width of the sleeve, width and height of the shoulder);

- position and configuration of the reliefs on the shelf and back;

- Width of board and type of clasp (single-breasted, double-breasted), diameter of buttons, their quantity, position of upper and lower buttons;

- parameters of the collar, ledge and lapel swing, their configuration;

- availability and parameters of finishing parts (leaves, pockets, etc.).

2. Develop a new model based on end-to-end design algorithm.

3. Determine the recommended size and height range for the developed model; Expand the range by harmonizing the proportions (jacket length, skirt length).

4. Create and print the model description, table of measures, pattern specification and table with calculation of pattern areas.

5. Export the pattern drawing and pattern drawing to a graphics program (Corel Draw). Form the drawings, make inscriptions, print the drawings.

6. Set the color scheme of the model. Export a drawing drawing of the model from Corel Draw to Adobe Photoshop in jpg format. Develop options for color and texture design of the model.

Technical means and manuals. Computer with installed program "Grazia" and algorithms of through design of suits of different cuts, printer. To perform tasks 5 and 6 on your computer should be installed graphics programs Corel Draw and Adobe Photoshop.

Literature. E.B. Bulatova, M.N. Evseeva. Constructive Modeling of Clothing, M., Academy, 2004.

Methodological guidelines

1. One of the most important tasks of clothes design process automation is to provide connection between the stages of model image development and design drawings.

In the Moscow Center of Computer Technologies for Clothing Design "Grazia", created on the basis of the Department of Fashion and Design of Moscow State University (now - RSUTiS) for the first time developed the basic scheme and technology of automated end-to-end design of products from drawing-drawing model to its curves in a range of sizes with all the necessary design documentation.

Cross-cutting design at the stages of drawing development and model design is provided by the following capabilities of CAD "Grazia":

- recording and execution of any calculation and construction process (algorithm) without the help of a programmer in a simple and clear language with the possibility of editing the algorithm   ,   accompanied by parallel

by displaying the construction on the screen;

- Using the database constants and variables required for calculation from the databases: general (e.g. values of dimensional features of figures) and related only to the described construction (e.g. values of additions to construction sections);

- description and execution of branching processes in CAD using the conditional "If" operator;

- Selection of any necessary fragments of the process of calculation and construction in modules that can be used in the design of various products, setting the required in each case, the values of parameters;

- Automatically recalculate and rebuild the drawing at any stage of the process when the values of one or more parameters change, as well as within a specified range of sizes and growths when the description and the drawing development process are completed.

To ensure a direct connection between the modeling and design stages, an end-to-end design algorithm is created in the system, which contains a description of how to obtain a parametric drawing of the product, the development of its design and the patterns of details. At drawing of the drawing-drawing, each parameter of the model which should be used at design development, is assigned a designation and status of a variable, the description of design process is made with use of these variables.

Depending on the features of the model in the drawing it can be depicted in different ways: by itself, worn on a dummy or on a human figure. The developed technology makes it possible to realize all these options. For flat cut products, such as men's and children's shirts, jackets, nursery products, etc., it is convenient to depict the model itself, without the figure. In this case, you can directly specify all the basic design parameters: the length and width of parts in different areas, location, size and configuration of finishing details. Such drawings-drawings with the designation of the measurement points of the product are also convenient for inclusion in the table of measures.

For the development of the model design it may be sufficient its drawing in one projection (front view), in two (front and rear views), in three (front, back, side). Sometimes it is advisable to give its view from the inside, showing where and which pockets are provided, removable buckle, etc.

To depict the model on a dummy or figure, the system created modules for building sketches of male and female figures (front, rear, side views), as well as dummies. Since often for a more obvious image of the model you need to put a figure in a certain way, for example, to put aside a hand or foot, created modules, the input parameters of which are the angles of the hand from the horizontal and leg from the vertical, as well as a module that allows you to bend your hand in the elbow, placing the hand at the waist. Created modules with different hairstyles, as well as modules that allow you to depict a woman's figure in the shoe at the heel (height of the heel - a given parameter).

2. The process of model and design development is carried out in different ways, depending on whether the algorithm of end-to-end design is created for the first time from the very beginning (2.1), the new model is developed according to the ready-made algorithm (2.2), or - by changing the existing algorithm (2.3). In the process of work execution, the new model is created according to the ready algorithm (2.2) or by changing it (2.3).

2.1. If a new end-to-end model design algorithm is created using the product drawing on the figure, the user shall assign a new name to it, load the base figure measurement system database and write down the algorithm content that includes the following.

2.1.1.1 Names of modules (called from the list), reproducing the necessary sketches of the figure with the values of input parameters (distances from the edge of the sheet and from each other), modules of the position of arms and legs (with the setting of angles). If the resultant setting of the figure is not satisfied with something, you can specify the parameters.

2.1.2 Description of the process of obtaining a drawing of the product with assignment of model variables.

2.1.3 Description of the process of development of the design and patterns of the product using variables assigned when creating a drawing - drawing model, and modules of the corresponding stages of construction (the base of the mill, darts on the waist line, performing methods of structural modeling, etc.).

2.2. If you create a new model of the same cut, which already has an algorithm for end-to-end design, it is sufficient to change the parameters of the original model (for example, the length of the product, sleeve length, the value of additions at different levels, width of the board, the position of the relief line, the parameters and shape of the collar, lapels, etc.). When the system performs this modified algorithm automatically reconstructs the construction drawings, patterns of basic and derived parts, as well as a table of measures. For example, Figure 1 shows a parametric drawing of the original model of the women's jacket, for which the algorithm is developed through design. Based on this algorithm, only by changing the

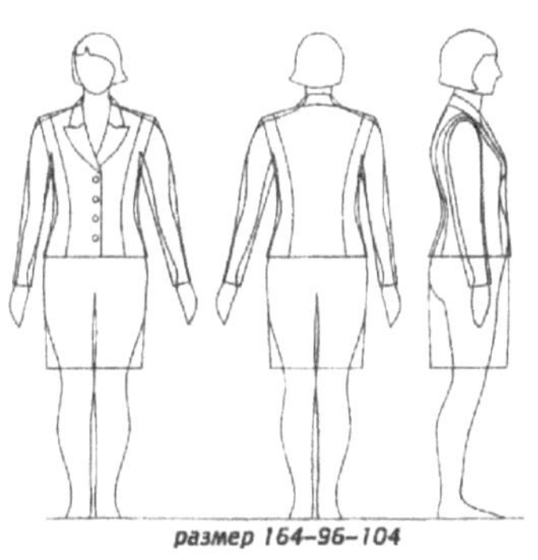

Figure 1

values of the parameters in the figure, you can get patterns of an unlimited number of models, common for which is the cut (the nature of the division into details): vtachnaya single-sleeve, back and shelves with reliefs from shoulder seams, collar with lapels. All others characteristics may vary (silhouette, the position of the relief at the shoulder seam and Its configuration, side width, the level of inflection of the lapel and the line of spread, the size and shape of the collar, lapels, the presence and shape of the leaf in relief, etc.). At the same time, the time of creating a set of patterns of the new model is mainly the time spent on developing its appearance in the drawing. Execution of changes in the drawing is done almost immediately, and the time of construction of the structure and templates - insignificant.

2.3. If the model being designed differs in the cut, for example, the reliefs on the back and shelf from the armhole line are provided (figure 2), it should be created on the basis of the available algorithm.

new original algorithm. To do it, you need to edit the model drawing and description of the construction

B

the example in question-

replace the names of the modules construction of reliefs from shoulder to armhole; make changes in the further description of construction (highlight contours

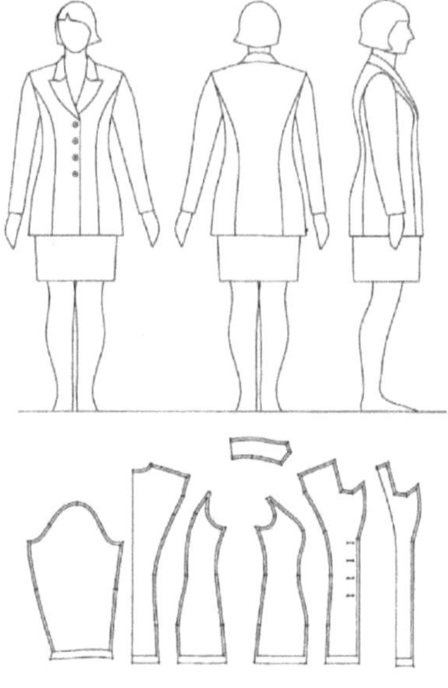

Figure 2

new parts, specify places location of notches, number of new parts in the set, etc.). If the model under development is a suit, which consists of a jacket and, for example, a skirt, then it is shown in the figure, and the parameters necessary for construction of the structure (length of the skirt, increments, etc.) are determined, and the name of the module describing the construction of the skirt is written in the text of the algorithm. Model features that are not taken into account in the modules fit directly into the algorithm, and if they can be used in any other models, they are formed as new modules. New modules can be obtained by copying and editing the existing ones.

3. Throughput design allows at the stage of model drawing development not only to work it out on a figure of basic size and height, but also to see how it will look

on figures of other sizes and heights. To do it, select the Reproduction Parameters option in the Runtime window and set the size, height, and completeness of the model figure you want to see in the basic size and height line, and the system will quickly automatically rebuild the drawing. The example is shown in figure 3. As a result, you may reasonably define the range of sizes and growths in which the model looks good.

In addition, there is a unique opportunity to expand the range by refining the proportions of designed products in different sizes and heights.

For example, a costume presented   at .
figure 1   ,   bad
looks on the figures shown in Figure 3.a. But the presented costume can be produced in these sizes, if you change the length of the skirt not in the way it is usual at the present time (with saving of proportions on length of the base size, without taking into account the change of width of the figure), but by harmonizing proportions at the stage of working out of the model drawing (figure 3,b). The skirt length found for each size and growth is entered in the "formula window" in a tabular form; the system will automatically build patterns of the corresponding length for each size and growth.

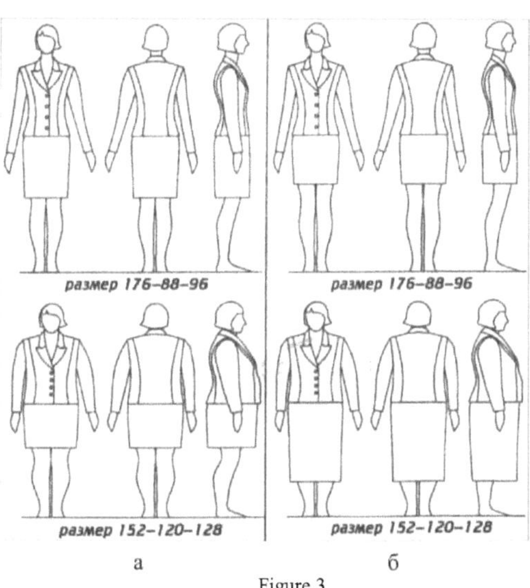

Figure 3

4. The technical documentation for the new product model includes: a model sample, a set of base size patterns or for the whole range of recommended sizes, technical description (TOR) for the model. The technical specification can be divided

into two parts: general and necessary for the development and production of the product at a particular enterprise. The general part of the PM consists of a cover sheet, a sketch (technical drawing), a model description, a specification of parts and a table of measures (tables of measurements of the product in finished form). To start the model in production, the table of measures should include not only the measurement values of the finished product, but also the measurement values of the patterns of the parts. Besides, for Maintenance the confectionary map is made, the areas of patterns are calculated, the patterns layouts, technological sequence, the table of consumption of the basic and auxiliary materials are developed. Technical and economic indicators of the model are calculated on the basis of these materials.

4.1. Drawing up a model description. The description is given in any form, but usually follows a certain sequence presented below. When developing a new model using the end-to-end design algorithm, the finished description of the original model is edited, as a new product of the same cut is created. Necessary changes that distinguish the new model from the initial one are made in the description. Table 1 contains an example of the initial and edited description of the model.

Table 1

Model Description

Model Description Scheme	Initial model description	New model description
Title (type), product purpose, material, etc.	A casual jacket for **middle-aged** women, made of **half woolen** knitted fabric.	An everyday jacket for **young** women, made of **woolen** knitted fabric.
Shape (silhouette), cut, clasp	**Elongated, semi-fitting** silhouette jacket with a one-sleeve sleeve, **central clasp for three** horizontal slitting hinges and buttons, with **narrow straight** lapels.	Jacket **shortened, straight** silhouette, with a single sleeve, **double-breasted clasp for two** horizontal slit hinges and buttons, with **wide** lapels.
Shelf Design Feature	Shelves with cut-off barrels, top dart translated into the seam of the relief coming from the armhole, and **finishing leaves in the joints of the relief.**	Shelves with cut-off barrels, top dart, translated into the seam of the relief coming from the armhole
Backrest design characteristic	Backrest with cut-off barrels, with reliefs coming from the armhole	Backrest with cut-off barrels, with reliefs coming from the armhole
Collar Design Feature	Jacket-type collar	Jacket-type collar
Viewfindings (sides, lapels, bottoms, etc.)		**On departure and the ends of the collar, sides and bottom of the product laid finishing line at a distance of 1.0 cm from the edge**
Recommended dimensions	The jacket is recommended for figures with chest girth from **100** to **120** cm, height from **158 to 170** cm.	The jacket is recommended for figures with chest girth from **88** to **96** cm, height from **164 to 170** cm.

4.2.   Specification of details and calculation of areas of patterns

When developing a new model based on the end-to-end design algorithm, it specifies whether all parts belong to the same class (i.e. can be located in the same layout). If some parts are extracted from another material, they are assigned to another class (for example, "main_pattern", "finishing_pattern"). After model creation, the "Create specification" option is invoked in the Model window. The window opens with the query: "Select the specification type:

Calculation of pattern perimeters

Specification

Area calculation"

The desired document is selected, viewed in the window, and printed.

Examples of the specification and calculation of template areas are given on pages 71 and 72. If a model is already described, it automatically appears at the beginning of the document. Documents may be directly printed or copied into a text editor for inclusion into the text of an explanatory note of a course or diploma project.

4.3.   Development of a report card of measures

During the development of a new model, based on the use of the end-to-end design algorithm, the table of measurements of the finished product (table of measures) created for the initial model is viewed and printed. The table of measurements of the finished product (table of measures) is supplemented or changed in case the new model contains or excludes finishing details, such as pockets, valves, leaves. The table of measures on the example of several measurements is given in table 2 and in figure 4.

Specification of m1209 model curves

Size 92 Growth 164 Completeness 2
Model author: Elena

Last modified 16/11/2009 at 12:27:48.

BasicSizeFullness .

921642

Minimum Size Growth Fullness 881582

Maximum SizeLengthLength

1001702

LECAL CLASS TOP

N	Name of the mold	Quantity
1	backrest	1
2	backspine barrel	2
3	shelf keg	2
4	shelf	2
5	sleeve	2
6	selection	2
7	collar	1
8	bottom collar	1
9	pamphlet	2

Just a mold of the top8 .

Total parts class top 15

LECAL CLASS Flyselin

N N Name of the templateNumber of the template

1 gasket_in_list2

Calculation of areas of patterns model AnnaSize

Increase in Completeness

961762

Model author: Anna Ivanova

Last modified 1/10/2005 at 12:06:00.

	BasicSize	Growth	Fullness
	96	176	2
	Minimum Size	Growth	Fullness
	92	164	2
	Maximum Size	Growth	Fullness
	104	176	2

LECAL CLASS TOP

N	Name of the mold	Quantity	Square 1	Square all, cm2
1	backrest	1	1515.1	1515.1
2	backspine barrel	2	780.3	1560.6
3	shelf keg	2	814.4	1628.8
4	shelf	2	1056.3	2112.6
5	sleeve	2	1450.1	2900.2
6	selection	2	747.3	1494.6
7	bottom collar	1	411.9	411.9

Only the top of the class 7

Total surface area of the top class templates6775 .4

Total class 12 parts

Total area of the parts of class upper 11623.8

CLASS CLASS Finishing cloth

all, cm2

1 collar1429	.	2429.2

Total mold of the class finishing sheet1

Total area of class finishing patterns 429.2

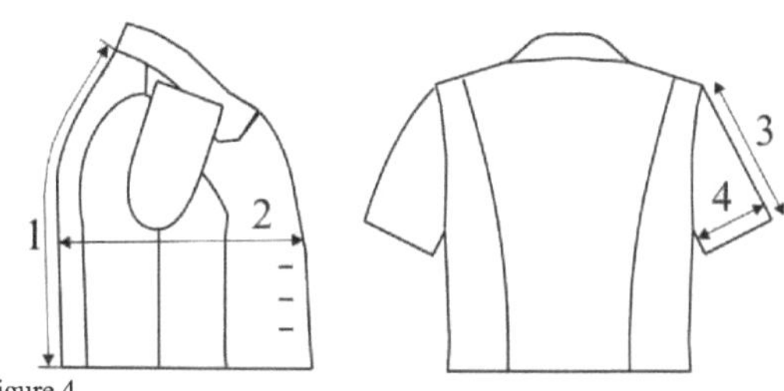

Figure 4

Table 2

Table of Measures

Model: female jacket Natasha

Completeness 2

№	Name	Growth	Size			Note
			92	96	100	
1	Product Length	164	54.9	55.0	55.1	Measured by
		170	56.5	56.6	56.8	mid
		176	58.1	58.3	58.5	line backs
						soothes
						collar to
						product bottom
2	Width products under armhole	164	54.8	56.7	58.7	Measured from
		170	54.7	56.7	58.6	mid
		176	54.6	56.6	58.6	backrests
						flanges by 2 cm
						behind the line
						opening depths
3	Sleeve length	164	43.0	43.0	43.0	Measured from
		170	45.0	45.0	45.0	culmination
		176	47.0	47.0	47.0	hose rolled up
						bottom lines
4	Sleeve width	164	18.0	18.7	19.4	Measured on
		170	17.9	18.6	19.3	
		176	17.8	18.5	19.2	pellet bases

5.   Preparation of graphic information for the MR or an explanatory note to course and diploma projects

Drawings from the Drawing, Pattern or Grid window of the Model window can be printed directly in Grazia. However, in order to make the necessary inscriptions and specify different line thicknesses, you can export a drawing drawing of the model and pattern drawings as a vector image to a graphic program (Corel Draw). For this purpose, having made the drawing or model window active, enter the "Algorithm" window, select the "Export to HPGL" option. A window will open in which the exported drawing is shown as well as a number of settings. In particular, the Export Settings window (shows where the drawing will be sent to), the Graph Settings window (where you can set the drawing scale, line thickness, etc.). There is a window where the name of the exported file is specified (corresponds to the sheet name on which the drawing in the algorithm is located). When several drawings are exported from a single sheet (e.g., the model design development stages), a number corresponding to the export sequence is automatically added to the file (sheet) name. After clicking the "Export" button and the System reply message "The strip (sheet name) was successfully copied under the name (the copying address set in the Export settings and the file name with the number)", the Export window shall be closed, and the Grazia program shall be minimised or closed. Then open the Corel Draw program, open a new sheet, select the "Import" option and call the created file. In the opened "HPGL Options" window, change the scale from 100% to the corresponding sheet size to which the image is imported. Fix image and regroup it for specifying of lines of different thickness and deletion of unnecessary lines or their sections (if it was not done in Graces). Form the image and make the necessary inscriptions.

6.   Setting the color scheme of the model.

Color solutions model can be set directly in the program Corel Draw, but it is most convenient to develop them in the program Adobe Photoshop. Previously, the drawing of the model should be saved in JPG format. To do this in Corel Draw select the option "export", and in Adobe Photoshop - "open as". Do not forget to replace the specified PSD file format with JPG in the opened window. It is necessary to develop several variants of color solutions for the model, including the use of different textures (Figure

5).

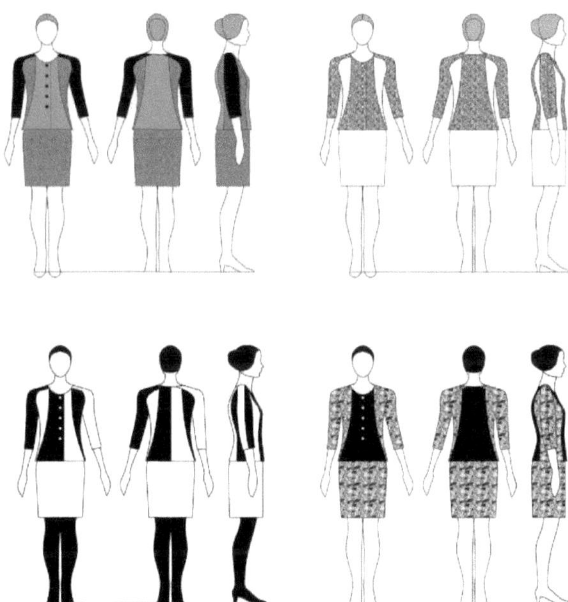

Picture 5. Color variants of the model

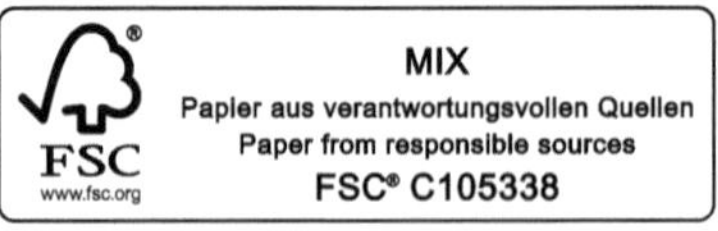

Printed by Books on Demand GmbH, Norderstedt / Germany